You Can Make A Difference In Silicon Valley

Simple Things You Can Do—Right Now—
to Make Silicon Valley a Better Place to Live, Work,
and Raise a Family

TOM HAYES

Tom Hayes
You Can Make a Difference in Silicon Valley
1. Volunteerism
2. Community Leadership

ISBN 0-9644598-0-9

Printed by Carpenter Printing in Silicon Valley, USA

AUTHOR'S NOTE

This book is dedicated to my children, Samuel and Elizabeth, and my wife, Debbie.

The idea for this book came to me when my son Samuel was born in 1992. As I am completing it, my daughter Elizabeth has already celebrated her first birthday. It is amazing how the commitment of parenthood puts one's life into perspective. I have found the arrival of children make two things enormously important: the community they will live in and the future they will inherit. Debbie and I have made a personal commitment to both.

You don't need children, however, to be concerned for the world we live in today and the world ahead. Whether you are a businessperson, a homemaker, a student or retired, employed or unemployed, high school drop-out or Ph.D., you have an opportunity to make a special commitment and contribution to our world. The thing to remember is that we own our problems and they won't get solved without our direct action. We can no longer hope that others—the government or the neighbor down the street—will take care of what's wrong. Citizenship means taking responsibility—and action—for the world around us.

WITH A LITTLE HELP FROM OUR FRIENDS

A project of this scope cannot be completed well without help. I am grateful for the substantial contributions to this project made by Ann Danner, Executive Director of the Nonprofit Development Center, and Siobhan Kenney, Executive Director of the Volunteer Exchange. Both know the nonprofit community well and worked diligently to provide listings of many organizations that need your help.

Critical editing and fact-checking were provided by Tami Begasse, Jody Kramer and Candace Lambrecht. Valued critiques and feedback came from the Honorable Jim Cunneen, Shannon Fryhoff, Joe Pon, Karen Hery and Joyce Milligan. Eva Burtscher provided an outstanding book cover design, and Jill McCoy did a terrific job with the page layout and typesetting. My gratitude also to Lori Smith of the San Jose Sharks and Teresa Holve of Valley Fair Shopping Center for their genuine commitment to community.

The book would not be possible were it not for the tireless, volunteered efforts of Brenna Bolger of PRx, the most generous person I have ever met.

Finally, I want to thank my mentor at Applied Materials, Jim Morgan, for teaching us all about good corporate citizenship and civic responsiblity, and my mother, Athena, for teaching her children to look for the good in all people.

Tom Hayes

TABLE OF CONTENTS

Preface

At Tandem, we believe very strongly in community service. We believe that positive change is brought about by individuals, corporations and communities working together to reach worthwhile goals. Each year Tandem's employees volunteer their time, talent and expertise in projects that make an important difference throughout Silicon Valley and other parts of the world.

There can never be enough volunteers. Volunteers make life better for others, and they make their own lives richer as well. With cooperation and a shared vision of how things can be better, anything is possible. That is why Tandem is pleased to sponsor *You Can Make a Difference in Silicon Valley* and put it in the hands of as many people as possible.

In this handbook for volunteers, you will find ways to help others and at the same time make your life more meaningful and interesting. All you need to do is give a small part of your time to a cause you feel is important. There are many issues you can help address—education, youth programs, job training, environment, health and fitness, the problems of aging and crime prevention are just some of the possibilities.

The role of the volunteer is important and rewarding. I'm proud of Tandem employees who donate their time and efforts, and I compliment those throughout the community who work to make a difference.

I would like to thank Tom Hayes for writing *You Can Make a Difference in Silicon Valley.* We can all make a difference.

James G. Treybig
President and CEO,
Tandem Computers Incorporated

100 HOURS TO A BETTER COMMUNITY

> *"Communities need more people who*
> *dedicate more of their time and energy*
> *and resources—more of themselves*
> *—to the commons."*
>
> —Amitai Etzioni
> *The Spirit of Community*

This book is about what you can do—right now—to make Silicon Valley a better place to live, work and raise a family.

The actions in this book do not require a lot of time or money, just a commitment to change things and make our community better.

Whether we realize it or not, each of us has enormous power and potential to affect change: we can make our voices heard and our actions count. As voters, employees and consumers, we have political, economic and community power. And, by working together, we multiply our power.

Our Community Is in Transition

Like all of California, our community is undergoing great changes. Tough economic times, an influx of new residents, rising crime and environmental concerns are but a few of the challenges to the quality of life in Silicon Valley. Jobs are evaporating, our public schools score low by national standards and gangs plague many neighborhoods. Without action, things will only get worse.

But who will act?

With a stagnant economy, tax revenues have shrunk, leaving state and local governments strapped for resources. Many businesses have been dissuaded from staying and growing here, and have been moving on to greener pastures. A rising number of residents are fleeing the area for better opportunities and affordable housing.

Who will act? We all must.

Working together as a community of citizen-stakeholders, we can take back our streets, invigorate our economy, revolutionize our schools and revive the great engine of hope and opportunity that has always been this Valley.

100 Hours to a Better Community

We each can make a remarkable difference in our community—and in the lives of our neighbors—by giving as little as two hours a week to one community group or problem area. Two hours per week is little enough time to be virtually "painless," yet adds up to enough time to make a significant contribution to a pressing community need. Over the course of a year, your time and resources could amount to one hundred hours. If we each choose one area to work in for one year, in 100 hours we can make a difference. By picking up this book, you're ready to start.

The opportunities listed in the following pages were designed for busy people like you. They are activities or tasks that can be completed in two hours per week, or in some cases, eight hours in a month (of course, you are not limited in how much more time you can dedicate). In addition, most activities include some front-end training, and in most cases the organizations provide all the materials and supplies you'll need to do the job.

A Citizen's Action Source Book for Silicon Valley

This book is designed as a handy reference for citizen action in specific, high-opportunity areas. It is meant to encourage you and help you find the appropriate avenue to make your unique contribution to our community. It is not meant to be an encyclopedic catalog of community groups or nonprofits. Many, many worthwhile organizations and efforts have not been included. Yet I hope I've given you the tools to locate them.

The book was compiled based on my own experiences as a volunteer and as the director of Global Corporate Affairs for Applied Materials, Inc., a position that allows me to work with hundreds of nonprofits every year. Additionally, letters were sent out by the Volunteer Exchange and the Nonprofit Development Center to nearly 3,000 area nonprofits asking for volunteer opportunities that fell within the 100-hours-per-year criterion. Through these combined efforts I have attempted to provide meaningful, impactful volunteer opportunities tailored to Silicon Valley's busy lifestyle.

If you don't find what you're looking for between these pages, here are two key resources to follow up with:

The Volunteer Exchange

(408) 247-1126 or (408) 683-9061 (South County)

(415) 965-2426 (North County)

The Volunteer Exchange is dedicated to promoting, supporting and facilitating volunteerism in Santa Clara County. Core services include linking interested community residents, employees and groups to volunteer opportunities in more than 500 local nonprofit agencies. As the focal point of volunteerism in the Valley, the Volunteer Exchange offers training in volunteer management skills, sponsors events and campaigns to promote volunteerism and works with local businesses, schools and organizations to encourage and support volunteerism.

The Nonprofit Development Center

(408) 452-8181

The Nonprofit Development Center supports all of the nonprofit organizations in Silicon Valley through a resource library, training and direct consulting. The Center serves nearly 10,000 individuals representing 1,000 different organizations each year. It also leads and advocates for the nonprofit sector, interpreting the sector to the rest of the community and working to promote philanthropy generally.

Chapter 1   REDEFINING CITIZENSHIP
Making Yourself at Home in Your Community

*"We're good at forming corporations,
not so good at forming communities.
The challenge of the '90s will be to go
beyond bits and bytes to make the
human connections."*

—Joanne Jacobs
San Jose Mercury News

It is time to come home.

For a generation many Americans have been gradually losing sight of what it means to be a part of a true community. In Silicon Valley, in particular, fast growth and career mobility have added to the problem. Today, most people who live in our Valley are first-generation citizens. Over 50 percent of the Valley's population either moved here or was born after 1960—the span of one generation. That "new-ness" can contribute to feelings of isolation and indifference. It takes time for people to put down roots, absorb and assimilate the conditions of locale and develop feelings of ownership for a community. When people are enfranchised and involved, they become active citizen-owners and their community thrives. When people do not connect, they remain merely residents, not citizens, and the community suffers in big and small ways.

Many who have come to Silicon Valley have yet to make the leap from resident to citizen. Either because they originally envisioned a transfer to the Valley as one stop in a globe-spanning career (and then ended up staying), or because they have yet to link up with an activity or organization that sufficiently stimulated them, too many people are actively uninvolved. A 1993 survey by the *Chronicle of Philanthropy* ranked greater San Jose 38th out of the 50 largest U.S. communities in charitable giving. A recent Silicon Valley Poll showed that only one in three people volunteer time to community service. That's well below the national averages and an indicator of a disconnect between our people and our community.

A Time for Passion

While Silicon Valley trails other major metropolitan areas in charitable giving and volunteer hours, you can sense a change in the wind. Everywhere you look people are putting down roots in the community; many young people who came to the Valley straight out of college in the past decade have begun to settle down, are getting married, and are starting families. New parents are taking an active interest in the local schools. Young people are taking an active interest in the arts. Many couples are doing good things for the community while making time to be together. People are getting committed to community causes with the same zeal and intensity they once reserved for on-the-job activities like new product launches and breakthrough research projects.

This trend is not surprising. Many people I talk to these days tell of a feeling of internal emptiness or malaise. They know there has to be more to life than work and play. They yearn for opportunities to do something as uplifting and fulfilling spiritually as work is professionally. They say they want to "give something back" or need to "round out" their lives. This book is for all of us who want to contribute to something important in our community—to give to something bigger than ourselves. The seventies and eighties were decades of inward focus, acquisitiveness and self-satisfaction. I believe the remainder of the 1990s can be dedicated to a renewed passion for action, community self-determination and civic responsibility.

Of course, it will not be easy to stir these sentiments within everybody. The pressures of today's world, the power of today's technology, the complexity of today's problems are forces that separate and isolate us. In Silicon Valley, we often feel overworked, unappreciated and pressed for time. Simultaneously, we are overwhelmed by solicitations for our compassion. There is a movement for every cause, an organization for every need, a crisis around every bend. Under this much strain, who has the time, energy or wherewithal to be a good citizen?

We do.

Being part of a community isn't free. There is a cost for the many privileges afforded us. It is the cost of ownership. We must be able to see that our world—our neighborhood, city, nation—is only as good as the care we invest in it. If everything seems to be falling apart, we have no one but ourselves to point to.

"I'm Just One Person"

Over the years, I've heard many people express some degree of doubt about whether an individual can really make a difference. "I'm just one person," they bemoan, "how much can I really do?" Plenty. Yes, it is hard not to recognize the enormity of some of the core challenges we face as a community, but remember, we created these problems and we can solve them. It is time to stop being victims of outside forces and start realizing that we have the power and the responsibility to take on even the toughest problems.

One key to remember is that we can no longer expect to solve the complex problems we face by:

- Throwing money alone at them;
- Paying someone else to take care of them; or
- Trying to go it alone.

The old African adage saying that "it takes a whole village to raise one child" is timeless in its wisdom. It will take teamwork and cooperation to raise productive children, keep our environment pristine and preserve our cultural touchstones. No one person has the time or money to solve an entire problem alone. That's not expected of any of us. But we can each do something. And, in the aggregate, the cumulative hours and efforts of all of us add up to an unstoppable force for change.

Community Role Models

We are fortunate in Silicon Valley to have excellent examples of individuals whose good works are making a powerful difference in our community. The most poignant examples are successful businesspeople and professionals who lead very busy lives, yet who somehow find the time to volunteer as community leaders. In writing this book, I was inspired by their commitment, compassion and courage: they are true role models and heroes for our time. By their example, they prove that we can all make Silicon Valley a better place to live, work and raise a family.

Richard Alexander

When others have closed their briefcases for the day, Richard Alexander is just getting started. After a day of handling projects for his high-profile law firm is complete, he then goes to work with numerous organizations that serve the public good. I have always admired professionals like Richard Alexander, who continuously and voluntarily devote their knowledge and their energy to improving their field in a way that will benefit a larger public. In this case, the beneficiaries are the victims of crimes.

Alexander is a San Jose attorney who represents consumers and small businesses who have been injured by defective products or dangerous chemicals or who have been defrauded by illegal practices. As such, he has dedicated his law firm to defending consumer rights and prosecuting class actions for consumers and small businesses across the United States.

However, Richard goes well beyond the limits of his practice in myriad ways. For example, as President of the Santa Clara County Bar Association, he gained recognition for agencies supporting crime victims' rights. As Chair of the Santa Clara County Advisory Board, he wrote a book entitled *Rape Crisis: The Victim's Rights,* a resource for victims of sexual assault which has been used as a training manual by rape crisis centers. As Chair of the County Data Confidentiality Commission, he wrote the first information practices law enacted by local government in California. In addition to all of this, Alexander has written extensively on consumer rights for more than 20 years, with hundreds of his articles and special presentations appearing in newspapers, newsletters and legal journals. He has also hosted a televised public affairs program and served as a commentator on legal issues for American Public Radio.

For his willingness to go the extra—voluntary—mile to assist people, Alexander has been awarded recognition by such diverse organizations as the Santa Clara Center for Occupational Safety and Health, The Women's Fund and the Santa Clara County Youth Commission.

Richard Alexander is a lawyer who through consistent service to his community far exceeds the law of averages.

Maryles V. Casto

Maryles Casto is the founder and owner of Casto Travel. I have always admired Maryles for her energy and spirit, which have not only led to her becoming a role model for women in the travel industry, but have made her a consistent leader and contributor in the community.

While building her highly successful agency—which is listed as one of the top 50 travel agencies in the United States and has become one of the largest privately owned corporate travel agencies in Northern California—Maryles has gained a reputation for philanthropy in both the Bay Area and her native land, the Philippines. Her management skills have been chronicled in books and magazines and are an acumen that she matches with a capacity for kindness, profoundly affecting the lives of people in her company, her community and her homeland. Her support for Bay Area organizations involved in anything from health care to culture is legend.

Maryles is on the board of the Children's Wish Foundation, the Committee of 200, the Philippine American Foundation and the San Jose Cleveland Ballet. In the formation of the latter, she had a critical role. Her introduction of the Ballet to

Apple Computer coinventor and cofounder Steve Wozniak was pivotal in the early years of forming the unique cultural joint venture between the cities of Cleveland and San Jose.

In 1992, Maryles became the first woman to receive the Asian/Pacific American Heritage Award from President George Bush. It was but one of many awards she has received as an outstanding business leader. As a woman who started a business on the proceeds from her jobs as a flight attendant and travel agency manager, she is a remarkable success story.

No less remarkable is what she has accomplished through her concern for people and community.

Pat and Joyce Milligan

When I think of the oft-used phrase, "an army of quiet volunteers," I think of Pat and Joyce Milligan, owners of the Milligan News Company. The Milligans are footsoldiers in this "army" who have marched along for more than a quarter-century, tirelessly fighting in the cause of literacy. Pat and Joyce have unfailingly returned all that they could to the community that has supported their business for nearly 60 years. People who give of their time, their money and themselves, the Milligans are devoted to assisting the young.

Pat is currently president of the Boys and Girls Clubs of Santa Clara County, where he devotes innumerable hours to promoting and expanding club activities. Boys and Girls Clubs has three clubhouses that provide activities for at-risk youth in low-income areas. Libraries at the three clubhouses are maintained by the Milligans' News Company.

Joyce Milligan has served on the board of the San Jose Public Library Foundation since its inception. Simultaneously, she is an active worker with the Literary Alliance for the South Bay, which fosters literacy programs in Santa Clara Valley libraries. The Alliance operates a hot-line service to connect tutors and learners with various literacy groups and co-sponsors the annual "Gift of Reading" drive to provide books to underprivileged children.

The Milligans are motivated by the importance of reading to overall survival of the individual in today's society—e.g., getting a better job, acquiring a greater sense of self-esteem. There is more. It is the pure enjoyment that comes from reading, which Pat and Joyce Milligan obviously know something about.

One of the greatest rewards of reading programs, Joyce Milligan says, can be that quiet moment when she is watching an adult who has only recently learned to decipher words read to a child.

Joe and Nicki Parisi

When I talk about contributing both time and services, the best example I know involves Joe and Nicki Parisi and their work with Valley Medical Center's South Valley Clinic. The Parisis are the founders of Therma, Inc., one of the largest mechanical contractors in the Bay Area. Joe and Nicki have worked to establish and maintain state-of-the-art standards at Therma in terms of how efficiently the company measures up in its industry and how warmly and compassionately it relates to employees.

The Parisis' compassion reaches well beyond their company, which is a reason why they include membership in the Valley Medical Center Foundation as part of their outreach. Through the VMC Foundation, the Parisis heard about the critical need for expanding VMC's South Valley Clinic in order to provide adequate health care for children in the area. They visited the Clinic and learned that its pediatric facility— built to serve 5,000 children—was serving 13,000. Immediately, the Parisis realized that a new pediatric facility was needed at a clinic where a few dedicated medical professionals ministered to a large community of the rural poor. They didn't hesitate to assume the responsibility for getting it built.

Building this $700,000 addition requires that Joe and Nicki donate their own time and resources as well as enlist the support of other businesses. Various companies have agreed to donate the building design, install the electrical system, provide air conditioning and plumbing and supervise construction. Organized labor has pledged workers. Proceeds from a series of fundraisers are also being contributed to the construction. The VMC Foundation was continuing to look for help as this book went to print.

The Parisis' commitment to the South Valley Clinic is more generous than most of us can afford. But their efforts have become the mainspring of a project that will require contributions from many and, in the end, foster a true sense of community.

New Habits of the Heart

How do we become citizen-owners of our communities? By recognizing what's at stake, by seeing and acknowledging how problems—even seemingly remote problems—are actually connected to us in the bigger picture. Eventually, we all share in the costs and the burdens of our community's issues. It simply makes good sense to share in the solutions to those problems on the front end, rather than wait until they have grown in scope and cost. There are ten areas listed in this book where your efforts can nourish and revitalize our community. You shouldn't feel compelled to do them all. The key idea is to integrate community service into your life as a new habit of the heart.

There are any number of ways to make a meaningful contribution to your community. In general, you can:

- Give money,
- Give away things others may need or
- Give your time.

All are important ways to make a difference, but perhaps the most important is to give your time and services. Why? Your time has a double value—it provides a value to the organization or cause you support, and it enriches your life by providing you with a rewarding, even profound, experience. Besides, if you volunteer first, you are more likely to also give money or other resources to that group (and you'll be more knowledgeable about what to give and how it will be used thanks to your participation).

If you have a skill, just about any skill, it can translate into a dollar value equivalent to a nonprofit organization. If you can file paperwork, repair computers, write press releases or provide even more specialized services, you are contributing to an organization the equivalent of $5, $10, even $100 per hour in costs they'd have to incur in order to get that job done. A recent Independent Sector study put the national average of volunteer time value at $11.58 an hour. Your time is valuable! You may not have the financial resources to simply write a check for $1,000 to your favorite charity, but you can still make that same size contribution—by giving a few hours of your time spread out over 52 weeks in a year.

Beyond that value to the organization, the rewards of service back to you are even more valuable; giving of yourself—your talents, heartfelt efforts, your emotional investments—provides a payback unlike any other endeavor. Doing something important feeds the soul and spirit in a way no material possession, career accomplishment or recreational pursuit ever can. And, as a by-product of community service, all other enjoyments in life can come into crisper focus. Work becomes more satisfying (that's why many smart employers promote volunteerism), family life is fuller, the problems of modern life are placed in better perspective. And community service can be, well, enjoyable.

That brings up an important point. Whatever community service opportunities you pursue, do something you enjoy—something you'll have fun at and become passionate about. That's the whole point. As Ram Dass and Paul Gorman write in their book, *How Can I Help?*, "The reward, the real grace of conscious service, then, is the opportunity not only to relieve suffering but to grow in wisdom, experience greater unity, and have a good time while you're doing it." The bottom line: saving the world can be fun.

Getting Your Company Involved

More than most regions, Silicon Valley is a community of employees. Many Valley companies deal with technologies and products that really are changing the world. That is heady stuff. Swept into the jet stream of that exciting mission, it is not surprising that people tend to identify strongly with their companies. It is also no surprise that we are often influenced more strongly by our corporate culture than our community culture. That's okay—the key is to ensure that your company culture places a high value on community service.

One benchmark you can use to measure your company's stance on community service and good citizenship is a list of commitments I've created, which I call the Silicon Valley Compact. It is a set of six policies or programs that provide for a fair standard of corporate citizenship in our community.

The Silicon Valley Compact

1. Our company shall include a commitment to "public service" in its corporate mission statement.

2. Our company shall set aside resources in a "community investment" fund.

3. Our company shall publish formal giving guidelines for the community investment fund.

4. Our company shall formalize policies and/or programs that encourage employee volunteerism during off-work hours.

5. Our company shall as a matter of course donate excess equipment, materials and supplies to appropriate community groups.

6. Our company shall measure its total contribution to the community annually.

As an employee, you can make a difference by encouraging your company to expand its presence in the community using the above "compact" as a measuring stick.

Finding the Right Volunteer Opportunity For You

After you've decided to open up your heart (and daytimer) and start as a volunteer, there are some things to keep in mind in order to optimize the experience for you and the benefiting agency. Here, the best guidance comes from the Volunteer Exchange:

- If an agency description or a volunteer opportunity looks intriguing to you, call the contact name listed and mention that you are interested in learning more about volunteering within the organization. The agency may offer to send you written information or may suggest scheduling a phone or in-office interview.

- When "shopping" for a volunteer job, it is recommended that you arrange to tour the agency, speak with paid staff and/or unpaid staff (volunteers), and learn about the organization and its volunteer program. You might want to ask about written volunteer job descriptions, inquire about training opportunities, and discuss your motivation for and interest in volunteering.

- As you hunt for a volunteer job, you can expect to be interviewed by agency representatives who are responsible for determining the appropriateness of potential volunteers. As a volunteer, you will be expected to complete the assignment you've accepted and perform the job to the best of your ability.

- Be patient—not every volunteer job is right for every volunteer. It is important to give yourself time to explore a variety of opportunities within different agencies. While one particular job may not be ideal for you, dozens of other volunteer assignments may meet your needs and expectations.

Sounds like good advice.

Chapter 2

THE COMMONWEALTH
Ensuring a Strong Local Economy

> *"The economy is a web of human*
> *relationships in which we each play*
> *critical decision-making roles."*
>
> —Frances Moore Lappé
> Paul Martin DuBois
> *The Quickening of America*

Why Economics Matters

It can be argued that the health of a local economy is the single biggest factor in the success of a community. Communities with sick economies show many symptoms of dysfunction: increased crime, an exodus of workers, declining pride. On the other hand, strong local economies are resilient to short-term problems, engage people with new opportunities, are confident and future-oriented places to live, work and raise a family.

A strong economy provides many benefits. It produces jobs, which allow people to buy things made by other locally-employed people— thereby producing more jobs. It generates tax revenues, which pay for government services, which produce a good place to live and an attractive place to open or locate a job-creating business. When it works, a strong economy is a positive cycle of events that benefits everyone in a community.

FAST FACTS

According to the governor's office, the average Californian pays $4,500 in state taxes:
- It takes an average of nine of those taxpayers to pay the salary of one public school teacher.
- It takes 10 taxpayers to pay for one police officer.
- It takes another 10 taxpayers to pay for one fire fighter.

For our economy to be sound and thriving we must ensure that:
- Residents can be productive and competitive;
- Our students are prepared for the work world of the future;
- Businesses can succeed in Santa Clara County.

What You Can Do Right Now
Improve Our Community's Ability to Compete

Every new worker enriches the overall economy, reduces the burden on government and adds to tax revenues.

► TEACH AN ADULT TO READ

In our highly educated, highly technical community it is hard to believe that thousands of people—many working men and women—cannot read a training manual, a materials safety data sheet or even a job application. Literacy is a basic job skill. When someone learns to read, he or she can substantially improve his or her job prospects, join the workforce and become a taxpayer—thereby strengthening the local economy in at least two ways.

For just a few hours a week, you can be a tutor to a new reader and not only change the course of someone's life, but give a sustaining boost to the entire economy.

Your impact: According to Literacy Volunteers of America, just 35 to 45 hours of tutoring can help raise a reader's capability by a full grade. Every adult who learns to read is better prepared to get a job or move up to a better job. As a reading tutor, you can start a chain reaction of success in someone's life.

> **Where to go**

Literacy Alliance for the South Bay
Jocelyn Guansing, HOTLINE Coordinator (408) 453-6711
Regional coalition for literacy providers in six-county area.
…YOU CAN tutor adults, inmates, people recovering from addiction, homeless children and at-risk youth in a variety of

programs, including basic literacy and English as a second language.

Partners In Reading—City of San Jose Libraries
Ruth Kohan (408) 277-3230
One of several volunteer programs of the City of San Jose Library system. Call the volunteer coordinator at your local branch or Jeanne Lo Franco, Volunteer Coordinator at Dr. Martin Luther King, Jr. Main Library at (408) 277-4822.
…YOU CAN tutor adults in basic literacy skills.

The Reading Program—Santa Clara County Library
Paula Hay (408) 262-1349 Milpitas or
Barbara Kong (408) 848-5366 Gilroy.
County-wide programs at all branches.
…YOU CAN tutor inmates, guests of recovery houses, expectant and new mothers; work on computer aided-literacy projects at various locations. Also, you can make classroom visits to read aloud to children at risk.

Books Aloud
Donna Coleman (408) 277-4878
Records and circulates books on tape to anyone with physically caused reading problems.
…YOU CAN be a "Pick and Packer," choosing and sending books for patrons, based on requests and intuition.

► GIVE SOMEONE A JOB SKILL

One of the major causes of unemployment in Silicon Valley is the "dislocation" of workers who don't have the needed skills to succeed in our changing company environments. Many hard workers lose jobs because they don't have the new skills demanded by a highly competitive world. That is a solvable problem. There is a need for job training in virtually every skill area. Whatever you do, there is someone out there who could benefit from your expertise. Put what you know to work.

Your impact: Silicon Valley's greatest economic asset is its workforce. When you raise someone's skills, you make that person more employable and you make the Valley's workforce more attractive to industry. In less than 100 hours in a year you can make a remarkable difference in one person's life, increase the tax pool and boost dollars spent locally.

Where to go

Ascent Employment Program
Art Lorenz (408) 257-8302
Job placement program for entry-level and above.
...YOU CAN prepare resumes, assist with job referrals, make donations of clothing for job interviews, help with seminars and make phone follow-up with clients.

Career Action Center
Jane Reed (415) 324-1710
Helps people find jobs and manage careers through training, resources and workshops.
...YOU CAN provide customer service support: research and develop contacts for the Career Action Network.

Center for Employment Training
Tony Bustamante (408) 287-7924
Provides vocational training, placement and follow-up services for under-employed or unemployed.
...YOU CAN teach tradesman's skills, building maintenance, automated office skills, English as a Second Language.

Central County Regional Occupation Center
Pat Plant (408) 723-6400
Hands-on training in over 30 career paths for teenagers and adults; offers elective classes to six school districts.
...YOU CAN teach resume writing and interview skills for placement; bilingual volunteers especially needed.

Center for Training and Careers
Irma Gardea (408) 251-3165 ext. 21
Wide variety of training, counseling and support services.
…YOU CAN provide clerical assistance, be a teacher's aide, or provide bookkeeping, data entry, maintenance.

Economic and Social Opportunities
Lori Ehrlich (408) 971-0888
Comprehensive, varied services from health to job training.
…YOU CAN be a mentor in the Placement Program—work from within your own company to encourage hiring and mentoring of program graduates.

Project Hired
Sandy Hurlimann (408) 730-0880
Assists disabled persons in finding temporary and permanent jobs for all skill levels.
…YOU CAN join the Business Advisory Committee; share human resource networks or technical expertise.

San Jose Conservation Corps
(408) 283-7171
Job training, education and community service for 18- to 23-year-old San Jose youth.
…YOU CAN be a tutor for a group of one to four students in English, math, life skills and/or GED preparation.

Women in Community Service, Inc.
Andree Patron (408) 292-8101
Screening, training, housing and placing for the Job Corps.
…YOU CAN volunteer for outreach recruitment; provide support for those on a waiting list; help find child care and transportation; and make referrals for graduates. You can also be a pen-pal—which can be done from home—or assist office staff and develop PR programs.

VTF Services
Marlene Kerrins (415) 493-1413
Trains and employs people with disabilities to provide landscaping services, do mailings.
…YOU CAN be a horticulturist: locate plants for landscape program; help disabled workers in landscaping.

Teenage Parent Program
Barbara Weller (408) 283-0763
Serves teens who are pregnant or parenting, working for a high school diploma.
…YOU CAN be a tutor and friend: help with schoolwork; build skills to help youth stay off of the welfare rolls.

▶ **HELP AN ENTREPRENEUR SUCCEED**

In recent years the legend of Silicon Valley as the nation's hotbed of bootstrap businesspeople has collided with the economic reality of rising start-up costs and lowering success rates. New business starts, one of the life forces of our Valley, are down in recent years. There are many causes of this decline, but one sure boost is to help new entrepreneurs start off with smarter business plans, broader resources, more critical advice and guidance. Every new business could have the potential to become the next Hewlett-Packard, Apple or Sun with a payback to the community seen in thousands of new jobs and millions of dollars.

Your impact: If you have experience starting or running a business, be an advisor to new entrepreneurs. A few hours of seasoned advice and counsel each week could make the difference between success and failure in a new enterprise.

| Where to go |

The Enterprise Network at Santa Clara University
Don La Haye (408) 554-6816

A networking institute that coordinates volunteers with over 150 small companies.
…YOU CAN be a business mentor to advise and network with emerging companies.

The Silicon Valley Business Incubation Alliance
Barbara Harley (415) 856-6990
Physical facilities for start-up businesses.
…YOU CAN provide professional and technical mentoring, as well hardware and other business equipment; help build a resource library.

► **RETRAIN YOURSELF**

Sometimes, the best way to help the community is to help yourself. The new global economy revolves around skills. Capital is readily available around the world, as well as technology and infrastructure. What differentiates one local economy from another is the skill level of the workforce—the ability of the employee pool to help a business succeed. In this competitive environment we can never stop adding to our skills arsenal. Each of us must see learning as an ongoing, never-ending process of acquiring skills that add value and advantage.

We are fortunate in Silicon Valley to have access to some of the best training and post-secondary educational institutions in the world. Many companies have tuition reimbursement programs for employees who successfully complete a training program or class. Adding to that, virtually every company today is providing an expanding array of in-house training in subjects ranging from specific technical skills to cross-cultural communications. Take advantage of every opportunity to learn something new.

Your impact: If you never stop learning, you'll never stop working. The higher your skill level, the greater your job prospects, and the more your labors contribute to a thriving economy. And the more skills you have, the more you can give back to the community.

Where to go

Please note that the phone numbers listed are the main switchboard numbers for the following schools. The operators will be able to direct your calls to Admissions, Transfers, Career Centers or special programs. There are also Adult Education Programs in most school districts.

San Jose State University (408) 924-1000

Santa Clara University (408) 554-4000

Stanford University (415) 723-2300

Golden Gate University (415) 442-7000

St. Mary's College (510) 631-4000

De Anza College (408) 864-5678

Foothill College (415) 949-7777

Gavilan College (408) 847-1400

Mission College (408) 988-2200

Evergreen Valley College (408) 274-7900

San Jose City College (408) 298-2181

West Valley College (408) 867-2200

What You Can Do Right Now
Help Make Our Schools Second to None by the Year 2000

There are numerous good reasons to help our public schools. In regard to the economy, schools are the feeder system for our workforce. High-quality graduates are likely to become high-quality, high-productivity workers. Investing in our schools is a high-payback proposition.

Our public schools are struggling with budget cutbacks, the rising costs of new materials and historically low teacher morale. We can no longer ignore our schools and expect a healthy economic future.

We need to revolutionize the educational delivery system in Silicon Valley and do it with the goal of becoming the best in the world for the 21st century.

▶ HELP SPARK AN EDUCATION RENAISSANCE

The boldest effort to date aimed at revolutionizing greater Silicon Valley schools has come out of the Joint Venture: Silicon Valley project. Called the 21st Century Education Initiative, this unique program brings together community leaders from all walks of life with the goal of preparing Valley students for the work world of the next century. The group's first phase is called Challenge 2000, and is aimed at sparking a local education renaissance—a new community commitment to build a world-class educational system that will enable all students in Silicon Valley to become successful, productive citizens in the 21st century.

Your impact: By volunteering to be part of a "Renaissance Team," you will work with teachers, parents and businesspeople to tackle some of the key challenges in making greater Silicon Valley schools second to none by the end of the decade.

> **Where to go**

21st Century Education Initiative
Dr. Glen Toney, Chairman
Carol Welsh, Executive Director
(408) 271-7213
…YOU CAN be part of a pioneering Renaissance Team in your local elementary, middle or high school.

▶ HELP CREATE HIGH-TECH CLASSROOMS

It is no small irony that Silicon Valley schools trail behind the rest of the nation in the use of classroom computers. A number of excellent efforts are underway to substantially rethink the education process, increase new technology in schools and equalize high-quality education for all.

Your impact: You can help network schools technologically, be a supportive role model for students, or participate directly in classrooms. By donating excess computer equipment, repairing or installing equipment, recycling software and other ideas from the following groups listed here, you can help your neighborhood school teach real job skills and increase students' productivity. You can also help awaken young minds to the possibilities of science and engineering through The Tech Museum.

Where to go

The San Jose Education Network
David Katz (408) 453-6748
…YOU CAN pursue opportunities in developing a computer network for schools, training teachers and students and providing industry support. You can also provide technical support for site implementation; train teachers and students; be an "e-mail pen pal."

The Computer Recycling Center
Mary Little (415) 428-3700
Recycles used computers and equipment for schools.
…YOU CAN help put computers and other technology in our classrooms by donating old and excess equipment for refurbishing.

Resource Connections
Irene Preston (408) 453-6532
Creates new ways for business and the community to be involved in the schools.
…YOU CAN challenge kids on-line! Scientists and engineers can communicate with teachers via e-mail to create challenges for kids in grades 4-12. You can also mentor students via e-mail in on-line projects.

The Tech Museum of Innovation
Julie Rose (408) 279-7175
A hands-on technology museum and educational resource for middle school students through adults.
...YOU CAN be an exhibit explainer: interpret and explain exhibits to school groups and the public.

▶ **HELP A STUDENT STAY IN SCHOOL**

Dropout rates in some Silicon Valley schools have risen at an alarming rate. A high percentage of all students still quit school before high school graduation. In our knowledge- and skills-driven economy, people without an education are too often people without jobs. While students make the choice to drop out of school for many reasons, many times it boils down to the lack of support at home and/or the absence of good role models in their lives. You can be a major influence on a young life. There are many exciting and unusual volunteer opportunities in our school districts. Most high schools have mentoring programs. Many schools also work with companies to provide field trips, teacher training and special projects. Call your local school district to find out what you or your company can do to actively participate. Some examples of existing programs follow.

Your impact: One of the best programs of its type is the Eastside Academies Program. Its "school-within-a-school" concept has an outstanding record of achievement in turning at-risk kids' lives around. Eastside Academies has a graduation success rate of 94 percent. As a mentor, in just a few hours a week you can change the course of a young person's life.

| Where to go |

Eastside Academies Mentor Program
Keith Bush, (408) 272-6443
...YOU CAN be a mentor to a kid who really needs your time and advice.

Mission-West Valley Educational Foundation
Darwin Patnode (408) 741-2165
Services for students include tutoring, book loans, scholarships, computers.
...YOU CAN be a tutor in this program and make the difference between passing and failing for a student at a crossroads.

PACT (People Acting in Community Together)
Kimberly Howard (408) 998-8001
The program trains leaders to take responsibility for solving problems and improving neighborhoods.
...YOU CAN be a Homework Center tutor and promote excellent achievement in after school drop-in centers.

▶ **HELP STUDENTS UNDERSTAND ECONOMICS**

Often our young do not understand money—where it comes from, how to make it. It is out of this ignorance that many students fail to see the connection between education, employability and a financially viable adulthood. Lacking that meaningful connection, already at-risk students often drop out of school.

Your impact: As an in-school volunteer explaining economic life in simple and entertaining ways to grade schoolers, in just a few hours a week you can make the economics of staying in school clear and possibly steer a young life on a new course.

| Where to go |

Junior Achievement of Santa Clara County
Debbie Gale (408) 988-8915
Provides volunteer speakers and programs to schools, focusing on the importance of school. JA offers four in-school programs aimed at students in junior and senior high school. Project Business introduces seventh to ninth graders to our free

enterprise system. The Economics of Staying in School for seventh and eighth graders is designed to demonstrate to at-risk students the value of school. Project Match, also for seventh and eighth graders, shows how math skills can be used to solve everyday problems. Applied Economics introduces the principles of economics and business operation to eleventh and twelfth graders.

…YOU CAN be a consultant, helping young people value education, stay in school, form good attitudes, be successful.

Project Banking—San Jose Unified School District
Linda Boule (408) 998-6108
Bankers come to the fifth-grade classes to teach basic check-book and money managing skills.

…YOU CAN, as someone in the banking industry, teach classes and take students on bank field trips.

▶ BE A ROLE MODEL

As they invent their lives, our children are always looking for role models. You can be a positive influence on a kid or group of kids just by being yourself. Talk about your own values, ambitions, career paths. Provide in-class talks, or participate in after-school programs.

Your impact: You can provide a constructive point of reference for at-risk teens who have few positive role models in their lives. You can give kids hope and alternatives to the negative siren call of the streets.

| Where to go |

Discover "E" Engineering Outreach Program
Santa Clara County Office of Education
(408) 453-6532
Discover "E" is a nationwide program to stimulate interest in mathematics and science and encourage students to pursue careers in engineering.

…YOU CAN be an engineering or high-tech role model to kids who might never know the joys of bits and bytes.

The Role Model Program
Betsy Galligan (408) 246-0433
The Role Model program brings business and community leaders into Santa Clara County classrooms to encourage positive life choices and educational achievement.
…YOU CAN be a source of inspiration and insight to kids who are at risk by talking about your career or business in a classroom setting.

▶ **JOIN THE FACULTY**

Remember a favorite teacher from your school days? Now you can be one to other kids. There are numerous classroom opportunities for nonteachers to support teachers in most school districts. If you have an interest, the opportunities to share with teachers and students are boundless. Participate in motivational training, help develop staff programs, organize field trips and provide other activities to open young minds.

Your impact: You can make a major contribution in the classroom by bringing your unique talents and perspectives to school. By helping teachers teach, you not only improve the educational experience for the students, you can increase the instructor's effectiveness and enjoy yourself at the same time.

Where to go

Berryessa Union School District
Pat Stelwagon (408) 923-1830
A public elementary school district dedicated to improving the learning experience.
…YOU CAN be a technology or library assistant: work with schools to update resources.

Business Education Partnership—San Jose Unified School District

Sheryl Stroh (408) 998-6119 or

Teresa Johnson, SJ Metro Chamber of Commerce (408) 291-5250

…YOU CAN consider a host of opportunities for you and your company to add to the quality of education.

Oak Grove School District

Judy Demko (408) 227-8300

Public school district with 20 schools serving grades K-8 in south San Jose.

…YOU CAN help students in the classroom with tutoring, doing art projects, working on computers.

Santa Clara Unified School District

Candy Holman (408) 559-8494

The Generation Connection promotes the use of older volunteers to help children learn.

…YOU CAN be an intergenerational volunteer: become a "sizzling senior," help put on performances.

Second Start: Pine Hill School

Barbara Benesh (408) 371-5881

Intensive academic program for those who have failed in other schools; prepares for GED.

…YOU CAN be a tutor/classroom assistant: work with students on basic skills; turn failure into success.

Wizard's Workshop

John McChesney (408) 296-4465

Provides science lessons in schools throughout Santa Clara County.

…YOU CAN be a storybook science assistant: help wandering science teacher with fairy tales and activities.

► **BECOME A PRINCIPAL**

Think running a school is easy? Think again. Better yet, try it for yourself. That's the concept behind the innovative Principal for a Day program. The annual event sends corporate managers and businesspeople to the principal's office for the day in order to get a first-hand look at the dynamics and challenges faced by today's educators.

Your impact: You can learn firsthand how your local schools are serving students' needs and what you or your company can do to support their efforts.

| Where to go |

Principal for a Day—San Jose Unified School District
Sandia Frank, Business Advisory Council (408) 998-6217
or
San Jose Metropolitan Chamber of Commerce
Teresa Johnson (408) 291-5280

What You Can Do Right Now
Help Improve the Business Climate

In bygone years, Silicon Valley was one of very few high-tech regions in the world—and far and away the biggest and best. Today, many communities around the world have replicated the benefits (workforce, available capital and technology, infrastructure) we alone once provided and are now competing for the same companies and jobs we are. Places like Silicon Prairie, Silicon Hills, Silicon Island, Silicon Glen (you get the picture) have become attractive, growing industrial centers—often at our expense. We need to be more conscious, as a community, of what we are up against and what it will take to keep companies and jobs coming and growing here. Bottom line: the more "user-friendly" we make our community to business, the stronger our economy will be.

There are also numerous little things we as individuals can do to both keep our dollars circulating within Silicon Valley and to attract new dollars from outside the area. Let's start with those first.

► DESTINATION—SILICON VALLEY

You can help attract visitors—and the dollars they bring—to Silicon Valley. You can market our visitor and convention facilities through your membership in national associations, clubs and organizations. Attendees of conventions and trade shows spend money on lodgings, meals and entertainment, which supports large service industries such as airlines, hotels and restaurants, as well as smaller entrepreneurial businesses. Even if you don't belong to a group or organization that can be attracted to the area, you can add to the visits of others by being an ambassador of goodwill; you can help by greeting visitors at the airport or being a "storyteller" to touring groups.

Your impact: The average convention or conference visitor you bring to the area will spend $830 per trip. The San Jose Convention and Visitor's Bureau reports $510,000,000 is spent annually by tourists. The tourist and convention industries have created 10,000 jobs. The Hotel Room Tax directly supports community arts organizations, sports groups and the San Jose Arena.

| Where to go |

San Jose Convention and Visitor's Bureau
Barbara Summers (408) 295-9600
…YOU CAN be a Silicon Valley Host at two airport booths.
Steve Hammond or Colleen Head (408) 295-9600
or
…YOU CAN be a host/storyteller guide for local tours
(training provided).
Joann Hirasaki (408) 295-9600

► TAKE YOUR VACATION IN SILICON VALLEY

Even though we often take it for granted, this is a beautiful area—scenic, historic, fun. Why not spend your next vacation—and your hard-earned dollars—right here in Silicon Valley? Check into a local hotel for the weekend, patronize restaurants and entertainment; visit the many cultural institutions and other attractions in our Valley. Discount coupons are readily available for many restaurants and visitor sites. And think of what you'll save on the cost of traveling since you're already there!

Your impact: Every dollar that stays in Silicon Valley to purchase local goods and services has a ripple effect through the whole economy.

> **Where to go**
>
> **San Jose Convention and Visitor's Bureau**
> FYI Line (408) 295-9600
> …YOU CAN get local entertainment and weekly "What's Happening" information.

► BUY LOCAL—BUY LOCALLY

When you buy something made right here in Silicon Valley or when you pay for a service originating here in Silicon Valley, at a point of purchase right here in Silicon Valley, many benefits stay here too. Buying local puts people to work directly. Buying local puts people to work indirectly. Buying local keeps more tax revenues local. The Office of the City Manager of San Jose encourages all residents to buy "big ticket" items, such as cars, appliances and computer products locally. About 1% of the 8.25% sales tax returns to the city where the goods were purchased, adding to the general fund paying for streets, parks, libraries and fire protection.

Your impact: Again, every dollar that stays in Silicon Valley to purchase local goods and services has a ripple effect through the whole economy.

▶ JOIN YOUR LOCAL CHAMBER OF COMMERCE

The chamber of commerce is the voice of business in our communities. If you are a small (or big) business owner or an executive with a company, join your local chamber of commerce

Your impact: Network with other businesses to keep our economic base intact and growing.

Where to go

Black Chamber of Commerce (408) 294-6583

Campbell Chamber of Commerce (408) 378-6252

Chamber of Commerce Morgan Hill (408) 779-9444

Chamber of Commerce Palo Alto (415) 324-3121

Chinese American Chamber of Commerce (408) 377-8228

Cupertino Chamber of Commerce (408) 252-7054

Gilroy Chamber of Commerce (408) 842-6437

Gilroy Hispanic Chamber of Commerce (408) 848-5780

Hispanic Chamber of Commerce of Santa Clara Valley (408) 298-8472

Los Altos Chamber of Commerce (415) 948-1455

Los Gatos Chamber of Commerce (408) 354-9300

Milpitas Chamber of Commerce (408) 262-2613

Mountain View Chamber of Commerce (415) 968-8378

San Jose Metropolitan Chamber of Commerce (408) 291-5250

Santa Clara Chamber of Commerce (408) 970-9825

Saratoga Chamber of Commerce (408) 867-0753

Sunnyvale Chamber of Commerce (408) 736-4971

San Jose Downtown Association
Nga Trinh (408) 279-1775
Promotes activities in the downtown area by sponsoring events and activities.

…YOU CAN be a special assistant: office duties include staffing information table, materials distribution.

▶ HELP MAKE SILICON VALLEY'S TAX AND FISCAL POLICIES COMPETITIVE

Today our communities must perform a balancing act: they must keep revenues in synch with the growing demand for services while at the same time keep tax rates low enough to be attractive to businesses (a big source of revenue). On top of that, the state's fiscal morass means city and county coffers are frequently raided to pay the statewide freight. In recent years, taxes have come to be part of the competitive problem in the Valley, leading to business flight and job loss (which leads to even further losses of revenue and the continuation of a negative spiral).

One organization that is working to represent fiscal sanity from a local standpoint in Sacramento is the Silicon Valley Tax and Fiscal Policy Council. The Council, another product of the Joint Venture: Silicon Valley project, is working to promote state and local tax policies that are both business-friendly and conducive to city and county revenue stability.

Your impact: As a member of the Silicon Valley Tax and Fiscal Policy Council you can help develop policies and legislative proposals that provide for both business tax incentives and fiscal security for local communities.

> **Where to go**

Joint Venture: Silicon Valley Network
Kim Walesh (408) 271-7213
Membership is $50 per year for private sector, $10 for public sector.

▶ JOIN THE SILICON VALLEY ECONOMIC DEVELOPMENT TEAM

Applied Materials Chairman Jim Morgan is famous for saying that, "business goes where it's welcome and stays where it's appreciated." That idea is central to the competitive environment for today's regions: in order to attract companies and their jobs you've got to do more than ever to be business-friendly. The exodus of businesses in recent years has had a negative impact throughout the entire economy. It was a key impetus for the creation of Joint Venture: Silicon Valley, a coalition of business, government, education and community leaders aimed at improving the Valley's economy. One of the most important initiatives stemming from the JV:SV process was the Silicon Valley Economic Development Team, a collaboration of business and government leaders designed to help preserve our industrial (and tax) base from further erosion.

Your impact: Contribute your talents, energies and connections to retaining and expanding Silicon Valley's high-tech industry.

Where to go

Joint Venture: Silicon Valley Network
Connie Martinez (408) 271-7220
…YOU CAN become part of a "smart team" to identify issues, problems or opportunities related to business retention and growth; work with companies that want to stay in Silicon Valley.

Chapter 3

THE BEAUTIFUL MOSAIC
Preserving Harmony in a Mulitplex Community

> *"Only by each individual embracing*
> *diversity on a personal level can*
> *communities survive. And only by*
> *integrating diversity into team building*
> *and quality efforts can corporations*
> *likewise survive."*
>
> —John P. Fernandez
> *The Diversity Advantage*

Why Embracing Diversity Matters

Silicon Valley is one of the most diverse communities on earth. People from virtually every corner of the globe have been drawn here for the opportunities and the quality of life. From Latin America, Asia, Europe, Africa and elsewhere we have come, and we have brought with us energy, ideas and passions that have enriched and enlivened the entire community. The influx of new immigrants will continue in the coming decade, and it will change the composition of our community. By the year 2010, African Americans, Asians and Hispanics alone will comprise 51 percent of Silicon Valley's population.

All too often today, the discussion of diversity focuses on the costs and challenges of integrating multiethnic people. This discussion misses the very positive aspects of diversity. As we face the challenges of a dynamic and increasingly competitive global economy, our diversity will be a strength—it is our advantage in the quest for community enrichment and well-being. It is precisely because we are made up of so many varied cultures that we in Silicon Valley can reach out and shake hands and trade with the rest of the world in a way less diverse communities simply cannot. Yet we must not permit our diversity to become divisive.

It is human nature to define oneself by what makes us the same as—and different from—others. It is human nature to gravitate to the familiar and the comfortable. In the bold, brave new world we are entering, however, focusing on our differences is counterproductive. If we learn from our rich diversity—of cultures, ethnicities, national origins, sexual orientations, physical capabilities and religious beliefs —we can become the archetype of the global community for the 21st century.

Whether we choose to make it a strength or not, we will be diverse. It just makes sense to use it to everyone's advantage.

Achieving Unity in Diversity

There are organizations for just about every ethnic group imaginable, from the Latino community to Sikhs. Each of these groups serves a valuable purpose. But the real opportunity is to work to bridge the gulf between differing groups by working in organizations and on projects that help us transcend what makes us different to that which makes us the same. The point is to increase the opportunities and quality of life for everyone without in so doing impoverishing the life of anyone.

Diversity will be our greatest source of competitive advantage and civic pride if we:

- Ensure that respect for the individual is a signature of this community;
- Create an environment where all people have the opportunity to reach their personal potential by providing avenues for education, recognition, acceptance and valuing differences;
- Support institutionalizing inclusive policies, practices and behavior within our public and private organizations.

What You Can Do Right Now

▶ **EDUCATE YOURSELF AND YOUR FAMILY**

The greatest threat to unity in diversity is ignorance. It is often what we don't know or appreciate about our neighbors that causes community disconnect and disharmony. The more you know, the more you realize that people all want basically the same things out of life: dignity, respect, opportunity, a better life for the next generation, and so on. And when you find that some people want something different, by educating yourself you realize that's okay too.

The best way to get to know new cultures and to reach out to new neighbors is by participating in programs that help raise awareness and sensitivity. In addition to their own outreach efforts, many organizations are making themselves more approachable to people who want to learn about new cultures.

Where to go

Go to the Library
Our city and county libraries have numerous sections containing multicultural studies and reference material. You can read about diverse cultures and learn to appreciate the similarities along with the subtleties and distinctions.

College and University Programs
Area colleges and universities frequently offer continuing education and not-for-credit courses in multicultural studies and cross-cultural understanding. Class offerings for professionals, such as "Managing Diversity" at San Jose State University, are also often available.

Cultural Events and Celebrations
From Tet to Cinco de Mayo, our Valley offers a potpourri of cultural events and celebrations that can raise your awareness for new cultures. Look to the activities or calendar sections of the *San Jose Mercury News*, *Metro* or any one of the area community weekly newspapers for listings of upcoming events.

Volunteer in the Public Schools
No institution is more diverse than our public schools. More than 30 native languages (and even more dialects) are spoken by students at a typical area school. If you want exposure to a

variety of different cultures in one location, call your local elementary, middle, or high school and volunteer two hours per week.

▶ **EDUCATE YOUR COMPANY**

While strides are being made to leverage the benefits of workplace diversity, we've still a long way to go. A most telling indicator of progress in this area is the admission by managers that things aren't yet humming. A 1992 survey by the Hay group indicated that only 5 percent of the 1,405 participating companies thought they were doing a "very good job" of managing the diversity of their work forces.

Your company may already understand the benefits of diversity. It may already have affinity groups and/or diversity training programs. If not, approach your Human Resources Department and open discussions about the productive advantages of such training and thinking for your company.

There are many "best practices" to borrow from other Silicon Valley firms. Many firms offer in-house or contracted courses on "communicating across cultures," or on "diversity sensitivity." Numerous companies participate in diversity working groups and conferences like those sponsored by the Mid-Peninsula YWCA. Also, many consultants are now available (most, but not all, are reputable and qualified) to help organizations maximize their diversity opportunity. If you have any questions about a prospective consultant, National Training Laboratory in Alexandria, Virginia evaluates diversity consultants and certifies those who meet their standards.

| Where to go |

Mid-Peninsula YWCA—Diversity Task Force
Lavois Hooks (415) 494-0972
…YOU CAN represent your company at the YWCA's annual three-day diversity conference, which brings together public and private employers throughout greater Silicon Valley to

develop specific action plans for better managing and leveraging diversity in the workplace. Ongoing seminars and meetings are available year-round.

San Jose Metropolitan Chamber of Commerce—Diversity Roundtable
Pauline Millard (408) 291-5250
The Diversity Roundtable provides an educational forum for the broad range of diversity issues that impact business and individuals.
…YOU CAN learn more about key diversity issues by attending one of the monthly meetings, or you can volunteer your expertise in the area of diversity as a guest speaker.

National Training Laboratory
(703) 548-1500
Evaluates and certifies diversity consultants.
…YOU CAN contact NTL to help ensure that your organization is working with a qualified professional.

► **EDUCATE THE COMMUNITY**

There is much we can do as individuals to promote and celebrate diversity and combat racism and divisiveness. Several excellent programs provide interested citizens with a forum and process to educate the community at large about these critical issues.

| Where to go |

Community Network
Kalamu Chache (415) 327-1994
ComNet is a collaborative effort of residential, religious and other organizations working to connect people, programs, projects and available resources throughout Silicon Valley.

ComNet is dedicated to building an inclusive, just and interdependent community by serving as a community-wide clearinghouse for a variety of projects.

…YOU CAN call ComNet and let them know what types of diverse volunteer opportunities you are interested in. You will be matched with the appropriate project or program.

National Conference of Christians and Jews
Lillian Silberstein (408) 286-9663
Part of a national organization formed to combat racism and discrimination, the local organization runs several diversity education programs in the community.

…YOU CAN be part of a Green Circle—a team of facilitators that goes into grade schools to talk about inclusiveness. The process usually requires four sessions with each school. You can also be part of the Experiencing Diversity program, which brings diversity training into high schools, colleges and businesses.

Interfaith Institute
Dona Smith Powers (415) 494-3093
Volunteers work together to plan cross-cultural/racial forums and events for the purpose of learning about and appreciating each other.

…YOU CAN volunteer to help plan events, speak at events, use your public relations skills to promote the institute's services, and donate resources.

Cupertino Diversity Committee
Lauralee Sorenson (408) 777-3195
Formed to bring the many diverse elements of our community together. The committee focuses on many areas, including education and business.

…YOU CAN volunteer for a particular program that interests you.

Santa Clara County Human Relations Commission
James P. McEntee, Director (408) 299-2206
The Commission provides information and referral service on
diversity issues and works to resolve neighborhood disputes. It
also provides staff for the Commission on the Status of
Women. Volunteers can take a 40-hour course of training in
order to become Community Mediators.
…YOU CAN volunteer to staff a conference on diversity or
other special topics, provide clerical support or make donations to the Friends of the Human Relations Commission.

Chapter 4

TAKING CARE OF EACH OTHER

Dealing with the Basics—Food, Shelter, Health and Peace of Mind.

*"If you want to lift yourself up,
lift someone else up."*

—Booker T. Washington

Why Taking Care of Each Other Matters

An embarrassment of riches plagues Silicon Valley. The Valley has the third highest per capita income in California and one of the highest median incomes in the United States (median family income for the City of San Jose is $54,000). And our wealth is conspicuous: our freeways are punctuated with pricey foreign cars, the streets of our bedroom communities are lined with expensive homes, our malls are filled with bustling shoppers.

All is not rosy, however.

Despite being one of the wealthiest places in the U.S., every night several thousand men, women and children in Silicon Valley go to sleep hungry, homeless and without hope. There are many working poor for whom health care is nonexistent. And many neighborhoods are under stress, resulting in families under stress. Why should we care?

FAST FACTS

- An estimated 30,000 men, women and children will be without shelter sometime this year in Santa Clara County. More than 50% of the newly homeless are families.
- There are only 2,083 shelter beds in Santa Clara County, and not all are available year-round.
- Contrary to the myths, most homeless are people who have hit hard times and who are eager to get back on their feet.

If you imagine a community as a system, it is easy to understand why each part must work well for the whole to run as it should. Problems in one part of our community invariably impact other individual parts as well as the effectiveness of the entire community. Whether these problems raise our taxes or create a drain on services, or simply represent the cost of lost opportunities, no problem goes without consequence. We own our problems. We cannot ignore or outrun them. We can only solve them early while they are more manageable and less costly (or we end up solving them later at a much higher cost).

Besides, the true measure of a community's decency—and ultimate quality of life—is seen in the compassion it has for its least fortunate members.

What You Can Do Right Now
To Help the Homeless

- Help troubled families "bootstrap" themselves back into the mainstream.
- Offer people the dignity, skills and hope needed to get back on their feet.
- Encourage government to increase the number of emergency and transitional beds in the area and available, affordable housing.
- Speak in favor of shelters at neighborhood and city meetings.

▶ MAKE A FAMILY "START-UP" KIT

When you shop, buy a few extra household items—laundry supplies, cleaning supplies, paper towels, light bulbs. Help your coworkers collect money to shop at a discount store. Look around your home, collect towels, kitchen utensils, cookware, linens, pillows either new or slightly used. Gather clocks, calendars, lamps and other things of which you might have "extras." Collect toiletries from hotels where you have stayed—save them for the kit. Call one of the housing shelters listed below to learn what families may need, then bring your start-up kit to help a family start a new life.

Your impact: Many times families and individuals in crisis find transitional housing but lack some of the smaller necessities and modest dignities of life. You can give their prospects for renewal a mighty boost.

Where to go

Emergency Housing Consortium/Santa Clara Family Living Center
Judith Bennett (408) 748-8622 ext. 24
A homeless shelter for families that also provides programs for children and parents.
…YOU CAN be a child-care coordinator: help organize volunteers who staff the child-care center on site so that parents can attend workshops on how to get a job.

Council of Churches of Santa Clara County
Nina McCrory (408) 297-2660
Coordinates service programs for many churches and faiths: e.g., housing, shelter.
…YOU CAN explore various opportunities available through individual churches.

InnVision
Antoinette Nguyen (408) 292-4286
San Jose's largest year-round shelter provider for homeless men, women and children.
…YOU CAN be a program assistant: help in whatever way suits you: in the office or with the guests.

Sacred Heart Community Service
Judy Romero (408) 283-5800
Helps people in need secure food, clothing, housing, jobs and education.
…YOU CAN be an English-as-a-second-language tutor: reinforce skills essential to success in our country.

Terrace Gardens
Denise Fore (408) 946-9034
Affordable housing for senior citizens, primarily in Milpitas.
…YOU CAN be an activity enhancer: help organize fun and meaningful activities and social events.

Vietnamese American Cultural and Social Council (V.A.C.S.C.)
Hao Pham (408) 441-6386
A multi-service agency serving the Vietnamese community in Santa Clara County
…You CAN be a Nutrition Program assistant: serve meals with dignity to needy Vietnamese families.

▶ RAISE THE ROOF

There are simply not enough locations to accommodate all in Silicon Valley who need emergency, transitional or permanent low-cost housing. Already an expensive place to live for those who do have roofs over their heads, for those without work or the means there truly is a housing crisis. You can help by working to increase the stock of available beds or housing units for those individuals and families who just need a little shelter from the storm.

Your impact: If you have even modest skills with a hammer and saw, or can paint, spackle or paper, you can help turn empty or abandoned space into usable living quarters for people who really need it.

Bay and Valley Habitat for Humanity
Bill Arnopp (408) 294-6464
Builds homes with donated labor and supplies for very-low-income families.
…YOU CAN be a jack-of-all-trades: manage the flow of information, data entry, mailings, word processing.

Community Housing Developers
Dennis Haines (408) 279-7676

Affordable housing for moderate- and low-income families, seniors and the handicapped.

…YOU CAN be a computer programmer or data entry expert to help maintenance department track repairs.

San Jose Shelter Foundation
Trish Crowder (408) 297-1737
Links people and organizations with homeless shelters needing assistance.

…YOU CAN be a Renaissance person: be a fix-it person or join a group of people to fix things, run errands. Also: you can volunteer to pick up extra soap, shampoo, toilet paper and left clothing from hotels.

▶ BLANKET THE TOWN

The cruel months of winter are hardest on the homeless. Wet, cold weather and long nights can be perilous, even deadly, to those who have no homes of their own. You can make a big impact by getting involved with an emergency shelter program during the winter. Donate warm clothes and blankets or help in a myriad of other ways that relieve some of the suffering of others.

Your impact: You can literally save the life of someone whose exposure to the winter elements could be fatal. Life-threatening hypothermia and worsening of other illnesses can be mitigated when you work to increase the number of homeless who safely get to a warm shelter.

Where to go

Emergency Housing Consortium Cold Weather Program
Laura Marquard (408) 291-5470
Provides homeless families, adults and youth with shelter in the National Guard Armories.

…YOU CAN be a resource advocate: inform homeless shelter guests about resources available to them.

Homeless Care Force
Robert Trefry (408) 986-0911
Feed and clothe 400 needy people using a mobile food van in four San Jose locations.
…YOU CAN be a food van driver/server: experience the joy of serving the neediest community members.

CityTeam Ministries
William Uranga (408) 293-4657
Free assistance for the needy seeking basic or emergency goods and services.
…YOU CAN be a truck driver or delivery person to pick up donated furniture and appliances and deliver to those who are struggling to make ends meet.

Pro Bono Project
John Hedges (408) 998-5298
Free legal services to low-income people, settling disputes, mediating.
…YOU CAN be a homeless advocate: help homeless people deal with government and other agencies.

What You Can Do Right Now
TO FEED THE HUNGRY

▶ **GATHER THE BOUNTY**

Food is a basic staple of life, yet an estimated 125,000 people—half of them children—seek food assistance each month in Santa Clara and San Mateo Counties. Hunger is a year-round challenge. Much of the food that we buy for our homes or that is used in restaurants and other commercial kitchens is wasted. You can make the most of what otherwise might go unused or discarded by collecting food for distribution to the hungry.

Your impact: Food donated to the major shelters or food bank is efficiently redistributed directly to people who need it. Every can, package or bag of nonperishable food you buy or bring from your cupboard—or every leftover meal collected from an area restaurant—will feed a hungry person.

| Where to go |

Second Harvest Food Bank
Beverley Jackson (408) 266-8866
The central clearinghouse for donated food in the county, linking donors and the needy.
…YOU CAN be a food sorter: sort, label and repack donated food for distribution.

▶ A CUP OF COMPASSION

Feeding the hungry is a daily challenge for area shelters and soup kitchens, which serve breakfast, lunch and dinner to an estimated 30,000 people every month. If you can work your way around a kitchen, you can help prepare and serve nutritious meals to individuals and families who will see the world differently on a full stomach.

Your impact: Few things can be more rewarding than serving a good, warm meal to a hungry person. By providing sustenance, you might provide just the boost a hungry and homeless person needs to start the road back to independence.

| Where to go |

Lord's Pantry
Martha Perez (408) 258-7563
Prepares and distributes boxes of food to the needy on the Eastside of San Jose.
…YOU CAN be a food distribution assistant: bag food, distribute it, answer the telephone.

Tending the Flock
Lilyann Brannon (408) 241-5769
Provides year-round support for homeless people. Every Saturday they provide 200 hot meals.
…YOU CAN become a hands-on volunteer by cooking, purchasing or preparing meals. Help the board of directors identify possible additional sources of funds.

The Salvation Army
Doug Jones (408) 975-2400
Meet the most basic of human needs, food. Provided without discrimination to all comers.
…YOU CAN be a "Go-Giver." Help feed the hungry by unloading and distributing food with a warm greeting.

What You Can Do Right Now
To Build a Healthy Community

While health care currently dominates the national spotlight as the debate over health care reform continues, there are immediate needs that are going unmet. An estimated 200,000 people in Silicon Valley do not have any health care insurance whatsoever. There are public health crises erupting anew from maladies long thought to be under control. And there are numerous public and mental health services that have been cut due to budget shortfalls on the state level. You can make a difference in big and small ways in the health of our community by supporting local care providers, by volunteering within organizations that face both growing constituencies and shrinking resources, and by bringing a modicum of comfort to those who suffer.
…YOU CAN contribute to the well-being of our community by volunteering at a health care facility and by working to raise awareness generally for health care issues. Regardless of the outcome of the national debate over health care, local problems are best solved by local solutions.

Where to go

Alexian Brothers Hospital
Dorothy Osborn (408) 259-5000 ext. 2201
Full-service acute care hospital serving primarily East San Jose.
…YOU CAN be a newborn photographer: photograph and footprint newborns; assist staff in nursery.

Alzheimer's Association
Karen Sortino (408) 856-1333
Supports Alzheimer's patients and their families and raises funds for research.
…YOU CAN be a family consultant: follow up with families that have been identified as being at risk.

American Red Cross
Dana Bunnett (415) 688-0415
Helps people prevent, prepare for and respond to emergencies.
…YOU CAN be a CPR and first aid instructor. Save lives by teaching classes of eight. Training provided.

American Diabetes Association
Carmelo Miraglia (408) 983-1288
Provides information and support to people with diabetes and funds research.
…YOU CAN use materials provided to heighten awareness in corporations.

American Lung Association
Danielle Fettig (408) 998-5864
Smoking prevention, cessation support, camp for asthmatic children, research, advocacy.
…YOU CAN be a Flu Campaign volunteer: prevent some of the 70,000 deaths each year attributed to flu and pneumonia.

American Cancer Society
Shirley Okumura (408) 287-5973

Educates public about cancer; provides services to cancer patients and their families.
…YOU CAN deliver educational presentations to public audiences about cancer prevention.

Aris Project
John Lipp (408) 293-2747
Educates the public about HIV and AIDS and serves people with AIDS.
…YOU CAN take people to appointments, errands, support groups, out for rides.

Arthritis Foundation
Diane Azzolino (415) 673-6882
Supports research and assists those with the disease to improve their quality of life.
…YOU CAN assist with annual Jingle Bell Run fundraiser (5K fun run), or in any way you'd like.

Bay Area Breast Cancer Network
Elaine Dornig (408) 261-1425
Trying to stop the epidemic through information, support, newsletter, advocacy.
…YOU CAN work with corporations to encourage education for employees.

California Institute for Medical Research
Dr. David Stevens (408) 998-4554
Biomedical research institute available to all scientists; discoveries are in the public domain.
…YOU CAN help devise and implement strategies for fundraising.

Muscular Dystrophy Association
Dana Mascali (408) 244-1210
Serves children and adults who suffer from neuromuscular disorders; research services.

…YOU CAN be a general assistant working on mailing, filing, and word processing.

The Palo Alto Medical Foundation
Patricia Amiri (415) 853-4703
Nonprofit organization that includes a Health Care Division, A Research Institute and an Education Division. Its main office is located in Palo Alto but the foundation has satellite clinics in Los Altos and Fremont.
…YOU CAN volunteer for both clinic and nonclinic support work. Volunteers are needed for the nursing support program, office work, in the libraries, for mailings and for special health fairs and events.

Pet Assisted Therapy
Marj Mason (408) 280-6171
Pets and friends visit children's hospitals, shelters, special schools, convalescent homes.
…YOU CAN provide general assistance to manage the program.

Planned Parenthood
Nancy DeWeese (408) 287-7532
Reproductive and health care services, education and counseling.
…YOU CAN make pregnancy prevention presentations in middle and high schools.

RotaCare South Bay Free Clinic
Sue Stadler (408) 778-6728
Provides free medical care to individuals who are unable to pay for basic medical care.
…YOU CAN, as a nurse, physician, social worker or interpreter, help provide care.

San Jose Medical Center Auxiliary
Candace Ford (408) 977-4549

Planetree Health Resource Center is a free library of medical and health information.

...YOU CAN be a library volunteer: welcome the public and orient them to resources. Bilingual volunteers needed.

Santa Clara Valley AIDS Health Services
John Avery Palmer (408) 299-4151
Through educational presentations, informs the public about preventing HIV infection.

...YOU CAN support educational programs and services to alert the community about the realities of HIV/AIDS.

Touchstone Support Network
Sharon D'Nelly (415) 328-4497
Supports children who have serious and life-threatening illness and their families.

...YOU CAN eat dinner with and play with children while parents attend a support meeting.

Valley Medical Center Foundation
Jon Driscoll (408) 885-5200
A private nonprofit foundation in support of the hospital and health services of the County of Santa Clara.

...YOU CAN visit with long-term patients, work with patients in rehabilitation, volunteer during at hospital fundraising events, provide clerical and office support. You can also arrange a V.I.P. hospital tour for executives from your place of work.

Visiting Nurse Association
Ginny Hoffman (408) 452-1854
Provides in-home care to chronically ill, frail elderly or recently hospitalized patients.

...YOU CAN provide comfort and care while relieving primary caregiver of disabled or frail elderly.

What You Can Do Right Now
TO FOSTER ABILITIES, OVERCOME DISABILITIES

People with disabilities really aren't much different from anyone else. They want to lead productive lives, enjoy friendships, make a family life, pursue their dreams. They do have special needs, however, and you can help. The most significant need you can fill is the need for friendship; take a disabled friend on outings, shopping, or just watch television together. You'll be struck by their special abilities, which tend to push the disablilty into the background. If you have employment opportunities or special skills, you can do even more and the rewards will be greater.

Your impact: You can dramatically improve the quality of life for a disabled child or adult simply by spending time, offering friendship and showing you care. Whatever time you have will make all the difference in the world.

Where to go

B.O.K. Ranch, Inc.
Justine Felahi (415) 261-1425
Therapeutic horseback riding for children and adults with physical and mental disabilities.
…YOU CAN be an assistant instructor: help a disabled person gain self-confidence and build stamina.

Capernaum Project
Nick Palermo (408) 286-3207
Recreational and social activities for kids with mental or physical disabilities.
…YOU CAN transport disabled kids in special vans to outings and recreational activities.

CHAI House
Ruth Rosenberg (408) 867-4724
Residence with 140 apartments for seniors and physically disabled individuals.

…YOU CAN do errands for residents who can't get out; bring joy and hope to others.

Crippled Children's Society of Santa Clara County, Inc.
Julie Duncan (408) 243-7861
Provides a variety of rehabilitation services to children and adults with disabilities.
…YOU CAN be a program aide, work in summer camp, day care, recreation, or any program you choose.

Gilroy Garlic Pressers Wheelchair Basketball Team
Robert Collins (408) 847-5571
Provides a sports experience for physically challenged people with a "need for speed."
…YOU CAN provide visibility for the team so more people can participate.

GRASP Foundation
Margie Monroe (408) 225-6134
Enhances knowledge about what it means to be disabled through information and education.
…YOU CAN, as a disabled person, share your life story with school-aged children.

Green Pastures
Audrey Dawson, Volunteer Coordinator (415) 965-2333
A normal, home-like environment for six disabled children where they are loved and challenged to develop to their full potential physically, emotionally, intellectually and spiritually. Continuity, support, individualized training and life skills are stressed.
…YOU CAN accompany the six kids on a Saturday morning outing, help with homework, play games, read stories. Offer specialized baby-sitting to other disabled kids in their own homes.

Housing for Independent People
Lynne Van de Bunte (408) 283-2209
Through housing and training, enable developmentally disabled adults to live independently.
…YOU CAN work one-on-one with a person who needs you to experience the joy of friendships, going to restaurants, shopping, to the movies or a ball game.

Jackson Hearing Center
Jean Ching (415) 856-0732
Special day classes for the deaf and hard of hearing utilizing an oral/auditory approach to teaching. The Center is part of the Special Education Department in Palo Alto serving Palo Alto children and in some cases children outside their district.
…YOU CAN volunteer your time in classes or for different programs.

National Multiple Sclerosis Society
Carla Hines (408) 988-7557
Dedicated to advancing the cure, prevention and treatment of multiple sclerosis. The organization educates the general public, people with MS and their families about the disease. They also provide information referral and peer counseling, have nine support groups throughout the county and produce a newsletter five times a year.
…YOU CAN volunteer your time and services in the office or at special events. If you have expertise in the area of MS, you can volunteer to be a speaker at one of their events. You can also suggest or help find corporate volunteers or donate funds.

Peninsula Center for the Blind
Susan Coan (415) 858-0202
Serves the blind and visually impaired in Santa Clara County.
…YOU CAN be the eyes for a blind person: do the little things; shopping; errands; be a friend.

PHP The Family Resource Center
Mary Ellen Peterson (408) 288-5010
A resource center for parents of children with special needs; service by parents to parents.
…YOU CAN be a "Kids on the Block Puppeteer." Use disabled puppets to help children accept disabilities.

Santa Clara County Special Olympics
Sue Rizzo (408) 267-2734
Sports training and competition program for developmentally disabled children and adults.
…YOU CAN be part of the Area Management Council and assist with planning and restructuring of the program.

Services for the Brain Impaired
Patricia Sanchez (408) 295-4119
Day treatment program for people who have suffered severe brain injury.
…YOU CAN train and retrain people to regain or develop skills; help them become more self-sufficient.

The Ark Center
Kathi McLaughlin (408) 266-8600
Private school for learning-disabled and emotionally disturbed children aged 6-22.
…YOU CAN creatively use technology to open new worlds of possibilities.

Timpany Center
Lisa Taylor-Babel (408) 295-0228
Aquatic physical therapy facility that services the disabled or injured of Santa Clara County. Center has several different programs for a variety of conditions and therapy needs.
…YOU CAN volunteer your time for special events, ongoing needs in different departments and fundraising bingo games.

VTF Services
Marlene Kerrins (415) 493-1413
Trains and employs people with disabilities to provide land-scaping services, do mailings.
…YOU CAN be a horticulturist. Locate plants for landscape program; help disabled workers in landscaping.

Westwood 4-H Riding for Handicapped
Nancy Couperus (415) 941-4808
Physically handicapped children ride horses to build muscle strength, balance, coordination.
…YOU CAN walk alongside the horse and help riders follow instructions, sit tall, and have fun.

What You Can Do Right Now
TO SUPPORT MENTAL HEALTH SERVICES

Some form of mental illness affects an estimated 100,000 citizens of Santa Clara Valley, including some 35,000 children. Depression, schizophrenia and other psychoses can strike nearly anyone, often without warning. Mental illness is no longer a stigmatized malady dealt with in hushed tones; much more data is available today to help communities care for those who are afflicted. Many victims can be cured through treatment and counseling and go on to lead productive, satisfying lives. Others, however, require longer-term treatment regimes and extended residential care.

While many new treatments are available, many Santa Clara County public mental health programs and services have been trimmed back in recent years as county officials struggle to deal with budget constraints. The reductions have impacted residential and outpatient care, vocational training and temporary housing. A number of private but largely publicly funded agencies have stepped in to fill the voids created in cash-strapped state and county programs. You can help improve the life of a mental health patient by spending time as a friend and by lending a sympathetic ear.

Your impact: You can provide counseling, service referral, support and hope to neighbors afflicted with mental illness. You can be a major contributor along the road to recovery for someone who simply needs what you have to give.

Where to go

Adult and Child Guidance Center
Darla Garvey (408) 292-9353
Providing mental health services to abused children and their families.
…YOU CAN help make the home safe for children by working with parents at risk of abusing children to build parenting skills and confidence to succeed.

Agnews Developmental Center
John Folck (408) 451-7689
Residential care and support services for 800 developmentally disabled individuals.
…YOU CAN work with residents in recreational activities, daily life training.

Community Companions
Teresa Jackson (408) 441-8284
Comprehensive support services to clients with serious mental illness.
…YOU CAN work with a mentally ill person to provide support and caring.

CONTACT
Barbara Joachim (408) 279-8228
24-hour crisis line: crisis intervention, referral, counseling, anonymous and confidential.
…YOU CAN be a paraprofessional telephone counselor and make a difference in your neighbors' lives. Training will be provided.

Miramonte Mental Health Services
Iris Korol (415) 617-8340
Helps people with mental or emotional disabilities fully participate in life in the community. Provides treatment and support services in the areas of employment, housing case management and counseling, residential treatment and in-home services for older adults.
…YOU CAN volunteer for a variety of positions either by working directly with clients or providing office help.

Chapter 5

VALUING FAMILIES
Preserving Our Community's Most Important Social Unit

"Perhaps the greatest social service that can be rendered by anybody to the country and mankind is to bring up a family."

—George Bernard Shaw

Why Supporting Our Families Matters

The family is the starting point for the good things in our world, as well as the root of most of society's problems. Today sociologists, politicians and social service providers are all in agreement—our families are under stress. The breakdown of the nuclear family is being identified as the biggest reason for the rise in urban crime and gang activity, the drop-off in school test scores, the rise in teenage pregnancies, and the decline of social values among our youth.

Why are families in peril? Economic conditions that require two-paycheck households, the growing number of single mothers, and the decline in government support to family services are among the most-identified pressures. In Silicon Valley, a high proportion of people who have only recently moved to the area exacerbates the problem: new residents usually lack an extended family support system to help them in times of need.

You don't need to be an expert to be a friend of the family. There are many ways you can step in and provide assistance to whole families, troubled teens, or lonely seniors.

What You Can Do Right Now
TO STRENGTHEN FAMILIES

There are numerous family service agencies in Santa Clara County providing support and counseling for nearly every kind of family or family issue. They need your help. Without these valuable agencies, which are always in need of funding or volunteers, our social fabric could continue to fray. You can help families in crisis mitigate conflict, solve problems and possibly stay intact.

Your impact: You can help preserve our community's most important social institution by bringing your energies, enthusiasm and compassion to those who need it most.

| Where to go |

Catholic Charities
Susan Alberto (408) 944-0282
Multiservice agency serving vulnerable, elderly, youth, immigrants, disabled, single parents.
…YOU CAN transport the frail elderly to appointments, run errands, go for rides.

Family Giving Tree
Jennifer Cullenbine (415) 326-1247
Provides food, clothing and assistance to the neediest members of the community.
…YOU CAN be a "Christmas Elf": collect and distribute Christmas gifts. Office jobs are also available year-round.

Family Service Association of Santa Clara Valley
Sofia Mendoza (408) 288-6200
Support services and counseling for families including domestic violence and drug abuse.
…YOU CAN take care of and befriend children while mothers are in counseling.

Family Service Mid-Peninsula
Patricia Williams (415) 327-0223
Counseling and therapy for families in crisis or stress.
…YOU CAN be a hot-line volunteer: be an empathetic
listener, provide information and referral. Training provided.

Jewish Family Service
Carole Siegel (408) 356-7576
Resettlement services for Russian émigrés, counseling and
vocational services.
…YOU CAN help Russian émigrés of all ages learn about life
in America.

Kara—Grief Support for Children and Adults
Ann Pursley (415) 321-5272
Supports individuals and families living with life-threatening
illness and grief.
…YOU CAN be a peer counselor: you will be trained to help
people live through grief and life crises.

Legal Aid Society of Santa Clara County
Liz Puga (408) 283-1535
Provides free legal services in noncriminal cases to those unable
to afford them.
…YOU CAN be an intake worker: interview prospective
clients, determine eligibility and need for service.

MADD (Mothers Against Drunk Driving)
Tom Satterly (408) 453-0900
Provides support and services to victims of drunk drivers;
works to educate and raise public awareness, lobbies for
tougher legislation.
…YOU CAN be the editor of *MADD Times*: help lay out and
desktop publish a newsletter of information and articles.

Multicultural Family Therapy Institute
Solange Cubie-Roca (408) 241-8010 or (408) 324-8287

Individual and family therapy to low-income clients, parenting and community-building groups, domestic and youth violence prevention.
...YOU CAN help the multicultural staff prepare and/or deliver culturally sensitive services to the community. Help new immigrants access and understand the U.S. system and services.

Office of Human Relations Dispute Resolution Services
Chere Montgomery (408) 299-2206
Handles all types of disputes, in schools, in neighborhoods, families, court referrals.
...YOU CAN be a grant writer: help win funding that would allow for increased school and volunteer programs.

Santa Clara County Bar Association Law Foundation
Rochelle McNamara (408) 293-4790
Legal services to underrepresented groups: children, mentally disabled, poor, AIDS patients.
...YOU CAN be the first point of contact with clients in mental health, children and youth; help with client referrals.

YMCA of Santa Clara Valley, Northwest Branch
Liz Gallegos (408) 257-7160
Serving youth and families; strengthening body, mind and spirit.
...YOU CAN be a "Newsletter Guru": edit, lay out, design quarterly branch newsletter.

What You Can Do Right Now
TO HELP TROUBLED KIDS

Kids today are under a lot of pressure—fragmented families, in-school and on-screen violence, culture clashes, threadbare societal values, doubts about the future. For some, special and often tragic circumstances can make their lives even harder. When no help arrives, troubled kids too frequently turn to drugs, crime or other self-destructive ways to express their hurt. You can help.

Often, kids in crisis just need someone to turn to, someone who can be a stable force to get them through the tumult they are facing. It doesn't usually take much in the way of specialized knowledge to make a difference; empathy is a key, and you'll be surprised how quickly your own childhood foibles and anxieties are recalled in the company of kids. Your experiences and ability to weather the storms of youth can be the best remedy.

Your impact: You can save a troubled kid from getting in trouble by being a supportive, caring friend and life role model. Many good programs exist that can help you connect with a kid who really needs you, make a difference and maybe recapture a life gone astray.

Where to go

A Place for Teens
Dru Barth (408) 354-3954
New facility where teens can choose activities and programs or just "hang out."
…YOU CAN be a snack bar supervisor: supervise teenage snack-bar workers, afternoons and weekends.

Adolescent Counseling Services
Lisa Friedman (415) 424-0852
Counseling program for youth at risk of drug and alcohol use, depression and suicide.
…YOU CAN be a jack-of-all-trades: assist in office, provide needed support to program staff.

Big Brothers/Big Sisters of Santa Clara County
Barbara Brodsky Jungert (408) 244-1916
Helps youth 6-14 and teenage mothers develop into productive, responsible citizens.

…YOU CAN work with a little brother or sister to help develop life skills.

Bill Wilson Center
Kathleen Hennings-Shield (408) 243-0222
Counseling, education and shelter for youth in crisis.
…YOU CAN be a recreation assistant, providing positive experiences for kids through outings and activities.

Cleo Eulau Center for Children and Adolescents
Karita Hummer (415) 328-2380
Works with victims of childhood trauma, divorce, violence, separation and loss, illness.
…YOU CAN be a grant writer: research corporate and foundation sources of support, write proposals.

Friends for Youth
Cathy Nafissi (415) 368-4444
Matches troubled youth with positive adult role models for friendship and activities.
…YOU CAN befriend and mentor a troubled young person: build self-esteem, trust and change a life.

Boys and Girls Clubs of Santa Clara County
Adolph Lopez, Executive Director (408) 293-8217
Now serving 4,000 boys and girls; operates three clubhouses in low-income at-risk youth neighborhoods. Provides after-school sports activities, library and study areas, health checks and citizenship training by self-government.
…YOU CAN serve as a volunteer at its fundraising events, donate sports equipment or computer equipment or sponsor a boy or girl for a year by giving $125.

Growth and Opportunity
Kathy Borchers (408) 779-1943
Provides subsidized preschool child care; free resources and referrals to providers.

…YOU CAN be a preschool teacher aide: work with Center staff to care for and teach preschoolers.

Optimists Volunteers for Youth
Tom Giuffre (408) 448-8683
Summer camp facilities and programs for disadvantaged youth at San Gregorio.
…YOU CAN be a handyperson: someone who can fix things, make plumbing, electrical, minor building repairs.

Parent's Choice
Earline Sweet (408) 270-5672
Residential program for young women transitioning from foster care to independence.
…YOU CAN be an outreach coordinator: help find donated supplies and resources for the program.

Palo Alto Community Child Care
Sheila Mandoli (415) 493-2361
Provides child care for working parents, infants through fifth graders.
…YOU CAN be a gardener at Ventura Community Garden: help children grow flowers, vegetables, make compost.

St. Elizabeth's Day Home
Hindy Ganeles (408) 295-3456
Full-time child care and early education program for low-income 2- to 8-year-old children.
…YOU CAN be a maintenance engineer doing general maintenance and painting the aging facility.

What You Can Do Right Now
TO HELP SENIORS

We're aging. As a community, we're living longer, often healthier lives, but we're definitely getting older. By 2020, one in five Americans will be over 65. In San Jose, the city's office on aging estimates that the number of people over 65 will more than double in the next 20 years. As we get older, we often need more intense or specialized services. Sometimes a little extra help can make all the difference in the world. Sometimes an interested and sympathetic ear is all it takes.

One of the biggest challenges for the elderly is isolation and loneliness. As our contemporary, fast-paced lifestyles keep family members mobile, and as the very old find that they've outlived loved ones and friends, there is a greater need than ever to build a support system for our seniors. Responding to this growth, numerous agencies have sprung up, both public and private, to help care for our older neighbors. Volunteer opportunities vary widely, with the most important attribute being a gentle understanding for the trials of getting older.

Your impact: Experts say that regular contact is one of the keys to a full and enjoyable life as we age. You can dramatically improve the quality of life of an older neighbor simply by spending time and talking, doing errands and simple household chores.

Where to go

The Bridge Counseling Center Older Adult Services
Nancy Escobar (408) 779-5778
Provides bilingual mental health services to Spanish-speaking seniors.
…YOU CAN help depressed elderly get in touch with life; write letters, run errands.

Cupertino-Sunnyvale Senior Day Services
Janet Hill (408) 973-0905
A center where dependent seniors spend the day in recreational and social activities.
…YOU CAN be a friend to seniors: share hobbies, stories, join in exercise or conversation to stimulate seniors.

Convalescent Hospital Ministry of Santa Clara County
Carol Haywood (408) 289-1581

Assures that residents of nursing homes have someone to talk with; someone who cares.

…YOU CAN visit with frail seniors, providing possibly the only outside contact they will ever get.

Friendly Visiting Service
Rita Baum (408) 296-8290
Visits seniors who are home-bound or in nursing homes and have no family support.

…YOU CAN share your life and bring a glimpse of the world outside the walls by making weekly visits.

Heart of the Valley, Services for Seniors
Glenda Cresap (408) 241-1571
Transportation and other services to seniors living independently in their own homes.

…YOU CAN provide transportation to take seniors to appointments, shopping, parties, or for simply joy riding.

John XXIII Multi-Service Center
Marion B. Johnson (408) 295-4116
Serves the elderly population in downtown San Jose.

…YOU CAN be a bilingual advisor: help the elderly from other countries meet basic survival needs.

Live Oak Adult Day Services
Alex Aranda (408) 354-4782
Day care for frail elderly and disabled seniors; many have had strokes or are disoriented.

…YOU CAN be a friend and develop close relationships with lonely, dependent seniors.

Morgan Hill Community Action Group
Sally Witmer (408) 776-1808
Helps seniors stay in their own homes, keeping them independent as long as possible.

…YOU CAN provide transportation, run errands, deliver meals, check in periodically, be a friend.

Outreach
Kathleen Alexander (408) 436-2865
Helps elderly and disabled people continue to live independently; prevents elder abuse.
…YOU CAN be a volunteer coordinator: with a head for management and training, you can change lives.

Saratoga Adult Daycare Center
Rita Pennington (408) 876-3438
Serves the elderly who are no longer independent and must have a care giver.
…YOU CAN be an activity assistant: share a talent, hobby, or collection with the frail elderly, play games.

Santa Clara Senior Center
Miriam Findley (408) 984-3266
Provides a day program for seniors who are dependent on others for care.
…YOU CAN help visually impaired seniors pay bills, do simple bookkeeping.

The Holiday Project
Cheryl Tannehill (408) 734-9055
Visit shut-ins, primarily seniors in nursing homes. Focus is on holiday season.
…YOU CAN be a "Holiday Elf": make the holidays bright for an elderly shut-in. Make a new friend.

| Chapter 6 | # THE VALLEY OF HEART'S DELIGHT |

THE VALLEY OF HEART'S DELIGHT
Keeping Our Environment Fit for All

"We have to recognize that we've reached a watershed in the economy, a point at which 'growth' and profitability will be increasingly derived from the abatement of environmental degradation, the furthering of ecological restoration, and the mimicking of natural systems of production and consumption."

—Paul Hawken
The Ecology of Commerce

Why Protecting the Environment Matters

It's our home. It's the air we breathe, the water we drink, the food we eat. We rely on the quality of the environment for our quality of life in Silicon Valley. It is too important to ignore. Many of our Valley's green areas are at risk, our drought-prone landscape is always a challenge, we have to balance economic growth with economic impact. Preserving the environment requires all of us doing our part, but there's more we can do.

The environment is the focus of many ongoing government and private activities. Nearly every government entity in our area addresses, or is affected by, land use, discharge of pollutants, transportation, water quality and conservation. As citizens, we can contribute greatly to these efforts by joining environmental organizations that are lobbying for or helping implement new programs. Silicon Valley could be a perfect example of high-tech industry and dense population coexisting with the environment, but we have much to do to achieve this balance. In just a few hours a week or month, you can help reforest our urban areas, care for our wild areas and wildlife and become a voice of reason in the debate over "green versus growth."

FAST FACTS

- There are 1,222,779 cars, trucks and motorcycles registered in Santa Clara County.
- 114,000 acres of open space—an area larger than San Jose—are at risk of sprawl development in the next 30 years.
- An acre of trees absorbs, in one year, the amount of carbon monoxide produced by driving a car 26,000 miles.

What You Can Do Right Now
To Preserve Silicon Valley's Natural Splendor

▶ **BECOME AN OPEN SPACE ADVOCATE**

The push and pull of progress in California, and particularly the Santa Clara Valley, has always turned on land use issues. The reality: there is only so much geography to this region—land use choices must be made carefully and with an eye to the future.

Many good groups have sprouted up to serve as forces for open space and wildlife advocacy. While some tend to get more political than others, the point is to make sure the public makes choices today—directly and through elected officials—that future generations won't some day regret.

Your impact: You can become a knowledgeable and articulate champion of our green spaces, wildlife preserves and hillsides by attending meetings, participating in workshops and joining in on field trips sponsored by any of the excellent environmental advocacy groups in Silicon Valley.

Where to go

Greenbelt Alliance
Nancy White (408) 983-0539
Protects the Bay Area's greenbelt of hillsides, farmlands and

other open space and promotes sustainable development.
...YOU CAN become an open space advocate: lead or participate in the Outings Program of bike rides, canoe trips and hikes focusing on natural history, farm tours and even innovative housing developments.

Peninsula Open Space Trust
Gretchen Schmidt (415) 854-7696
Acquires, preserves and protects open space in Santa Clara and San Mateo Counties, working with city and county governments, the community and private citizens.
...YOU CAN, as an experienced sales representative, market P.O.S.T. notecards for visibility and fundraising. You can also be an exhibit coordinator for community events.

Peninsula Conservation Center
Joan van Gelder (415) 962-9876
Promotes and enables local environmental action, providing reliable, balanced information.
...YOU CAN be the Information Desk manager: greet visitors, answer phones, answer questions, assist staff.

The Trail Center
Joan Schwan (415) 968-7065
Volunteer trail building and maintenance projects foster land stewardship.
...YOU CAN research sources of funds and extend the reach of the Trail Center.

United New Conservationists
Lilyann Brannon (408) 241-5769
Focus on preserving urban open space, such as community gardens; monitor changes in land use policy.
...YOU CAN be a membership coordinator: prepare membership letters, follow up; assign members to committees.

▶ BACK TO THE GARDEN

Protecting our natural places is important; so is preserving and maintaining them. There are some 60,000 acres of park and open space preserve lands in and around Santa Clara Valley, and too few government resources to adequately tend to them all. Trails need to be maintained, brush cut back for fire safety purposes, park areas cleaned and spruced up. You can also work at park stations and with park rangers giving tours and talks on the grounds. Bottom line is, there are many opportunities for each of us to spend a weekend morning or two in the splendor of natural foothills, wetlands and forests working to preserve our ecological heritage and future.

Your impact: Silicon Valley's parks and open spaces are a community treasure. By working a few hours a week as a trail or park volunteer, in inner-city parks or in wildlife preserves or recreation areas, you can help keep our treasure safe for generations to come.

Where to go

Adopt-A-Park
Elizabeth Neves (408) 277-4477
Volunteers provide for the overall maintenance of parks throughout the City of San Jose and other area cities.
…YOU CAN take care of your neighborhood park with friends and neighbors.

Bay Area Action
Laura Stec (415) 321-1994
Education organization working to preserve and restore the environment. Sponsors several different education projects.
…YOU CAN be an organic gardening assistant: plant, weed and water. Build fencing around premises.

City of San Jose Prusch Farm Park
Cindy Rebhan (408) 926-5555
Helps inner-city kids learn the value of animals, plants and the environment.

…YOU CAN be a tour docent: explain to children where their food, clothing, even toys come from.

Environmental Volunteers
Irene Estelle (415) 961-0545
Helps K-8 students develop responsibility for and understanding of the environment.
…YOU CAN be an education docent: teach hands-on natural science classes; lead field trips; develop responsible citizens.

Hidden Villa
Minka Van der Zwaag (415) 949-8655
Fosters respect for human dignity and diversity and the protection of the environment.
…YOU CAN be an environment education guide: lead school groups on tours of the wonderful farm.

Volunteer Saratoga
Carrie Deane (408) 867-3438 ext. 252
Coordinates all of the volunteer efforts for the City of Saratoga.
…YOU CAN adopt a park. Volunteers spruce up the park, do general litter clean-up, painting and weeding.

▶ **PLANT SEEDS FOR THE FUTURE**

Trees provide more than shade. They help clean the air, prevent topsoil erosion, and protect our water supplies. The Santa Clara Valley is home to many varieties of indigenous trees—from the tiny crape myrtle to the majestic redwoods. The problem is, as the Valley becomes increasingly urbanized, we need more of all types of trees. And we need to protect and refresh the trees we already have from the rigors of urban realities: asphalt-compacted soil chokes tree roots of air and nutrients; airborne pollutants damage leaves.

Reforestation and refoliation projects have been underway in recent years to help people of all walks of life become modern-day

"Johnny Appleseeds." You can be part of a weekend planting project, or you can rally a group of friends or coworkers to take on a planting project.

Your impact: Help plant and care for life-giving trees throughout Silicon Valley's urban landscape. In just a few weekend hours, you can be part of the regreening process that will harvest years of benefits for us all.

Where to go

Our City Forest
Beth Stochaj (408) 277-3969
Helps schools, neighborhood groups and service clubs plant and care for trees.
…YOU CAN be a "Tree Amigo": help groups plant and care for trees and "regreen" the cities.

San Jose Beautiful
Margaret Wagenet (408) 277-5208
Environmental education, landscaping and beautification projects in San Jose.
…YOU CAN coordinate volunteers throughout the year for events and festivals.

San Jose Conservation Corps
Theresa Tran (408) 283-7171 or 283-7174
Nonprofit program that prepares youth for employment through its job training. Corps members install fences, plant and replace trees and clean up creeks.
…YOU CAN volunteer as a tutor for education classes and provide resources to keep the program growing.

What You Can Do Right Now
To Reduce Air and Water Pollution

▶ **GET OFF THE ROAD**

Automobiles are one of the biggest sources of air pollution—30 percent of the deadly carbon dioxide spewed into the Bay Area air and 70 percent of the carbon monoxide we breathe comes from automobile exhausts. Other nasty elements, like hydrocarbons, nitrogen oxides and ozone, also complicate the purity of the air we rely on for life.

The best way to keep heavy metals and other pollutants out of our air supply is to keep people out of their cars and off the road. You can make a difference by using any alternative to driving alone: carpool, vanpool, take public transit, ride a bike, walk if you can. Also, tune up your car, keep tires properly inflated and use the air conditioning sparingly.

Your impact: According to the Environmental Protection Agency, you can keep up to 10,562 pounds of pollution per year out of the air for every car you keep off the road, not to mention saving fuel, time (on average) and lives in the process. Sharing a ride (carpooling or using public transit) just one day a week would reduce traffic, pollution and parking problems by 20 percent.

| Where to go |

RIDES
(800) 755-7665
Bay Area-wide carpool network and information about ride-sharing. In its first 14 years, RIDES has contributed to keeping 26,600 tons of pollution from being poured into the atmosphere and saved 53 million gallons of fuel.
…YOU CAN stop riding alone and start breathing easier.

Silicon Valley Bicycle Coalition
Bill Michel (415) 965-8456
Works for safety, adequate parking and improved conditions for cyclers.

…YOU CAN be a bicycling advocate or be a bicycle valet parking attendant: help park bicycles at local art and wine festivals.

▶ **PHONE IT IN**

One idea for keeping cars off the road that is gaining in popularity is to increase the number of employees who "telecommute" to work, instead of driving. Smart Valley, Inc.—another offshoot of the Joint Venture: Silicon Valley Network—defines telecommuting as "the partial or total substitution of telecommunications technology for the trip to and from the primary workplace…simply put, it's moving the work to the workers instead of the workers to work."

Today's technology—computers, modems, fax machines, cellular phones and advanced communications links—have made it much easier to imagine a world where some employees will no longer need to be tethered to a company workspace.

There are, however, many open issues relating to telecommuting. It's clearly not suited for all types of work, nor for all types of companies. If you'd like to explore the telecommute option and all it entails, Smart Valley has recently published a Telecommuting Guide, which walks individuals and companies through the entire process.

Your impact: If even a modest percentage of the Bay Area's 3.1 million workers telecommuted one day per week, it would substantially reduce traffic, pollution and parking problems for all of us.

| Where to go |

Smart Valley, Inc.
(415) 843-2160
Working to create an electronic community by developing an advanced information infrastructure and the collective ability to use it.
…YOU CAN volunteer your services or make a contribution to the Smart Valley Charitable Fund.

What You Can Do Right Now
To Help Local Wildlife

► GOOD HABITATS

Quantum engineers, software writers and biochemists aren't the only exotic inhabitants of Santa Clara Valley. The area is also home to a wide variety of native wildlife, such as coyotes, mountain lions, owls, opossums and many types of waterfowl and shorebirds. Urbanization has encroached on some natural habitats, but many important areas have been preserved unspoiled and are excellent community resources. These areas need to be kept up. Also, animals that occasionally stray from their protected environments, and some that don't, can become injured or ill. We humans can help. With a little bit of training, you can help save and make well again a hurting animal that can then return to the wild.

Your impact: The need to repair and maintain, upgrade and improve Santa Clara Valley's natural environs is an ongoing concern with little in the way of public financial underwriting. You can help keep the home grounds of our animal friends safe and thriving by working as a trail worker, animal rescuer or general advocate for the preservation of natural habitats.

Where to go

Companion Animal Rescue Effort
Ellen Prior (408) 227-2273
Foster care placement for homeless cats/dogs; advises on animal care and spaying/neutering.
…YOU CAN provide a foster home for a pet while a permanent, stable, loving new home is found.

Palo Alto Animal Services
Susie Brain (415) 329-2189
Municipal animal shelter and spay and neuter clinic.

…YOU CAN be an animal birth control counselor: advise pet owners of the benefits of pet birth control.

San Franciso Bay Bird Observatory
Janet Hanson (408) 946-6548
Monitors bird population of South San Francisco Bay, reports to government agencies.
…YOU CAN be an avian population monitor. Assist staff in conducting field studies of local birds.

Santa Clara County Parks and Recreation Department
Martha Heutel (408) 358-3741
Provides parklands and open space for the enjoyment of County residents and visitors.
…YOU CAN be a park volunteer. Work as a trail worker (repairing trails), docent or trail watcher (monitor).

Shoreline at Mountain View
Ginny Kaminski (415) 903-6073
Shoreline is a recreational and wildlife area next to San Francisco Bay.
…YOU CAN be a volunteer ranger providing visitor information at the main gatehouse/entrance to Shoreline.

South Bay in Defense of Animals
E.J. Meininger (408) 927-9281
Educate the public that we share the planet with other species, we don't own them.
…YOU CAN be an Animal Advocate: write letters to legislators, Congress promoting respect for animals.

Wildlife Education and Rehabilitation Center
Sue Howell (408) 779-WERC
Rehabilitates injured wildlife and educates the community for peaceful coexistence.
…YOU CAN be a wildlife rehabilitator and handler: work with wild creatures in educational programs.

Wildlife Rescue
Laura Pitts (415) 494-7417
Resource for wildlife rehabilitation and to promote under-
standing of wildlife.
…YOU CAN be wildlife rehabilitator: feed and care for
orphaned or injured birds and small animals.

Youth Science Institute
Three locations:
Alum Rock Park in San Jose (408) 258-4322
Vasona Park in Los Gatos (408) 356-4945
Sanborne-Skyline Park in Saratoga (408) 867-6940
Dedicated to enriching the community through science and
environmental education. Offers a variety of wildlife rescue
and environmental programs.
…YOU CAN call up any of the three facilities and volunteer
for their different programs.

What You Can Do Right Now
To Promote Environmental Action

▶ BE A FRIEND OF THE EARTH

If we want to keep our world clean, beautiful and self-renewing, we'll
have to do more than celebrate Earth Day once a year. Environmental
action can be made a part of everybody's lifestyle. Already around
the Valley, recycling and waste reduction programs are becoming com-
monplace (San Jose's curbside recycling program has quickly become
a national model). But raising consciousness and educating people
takes more—it takes information, a grasp of the implications and a
handle on the solutions. You can become an educated, forceful champion of the environment by joining any one of several leading
environmental advocacy organizations located in Santa Clara Valley.

Your impact: Armed with current information and the ability to communicate both challenges and opportunities, you can become a true friend of the earth. Every action you take will have a direct impact on the restoration and preservation of the only home we have.

Where to go

Chinese American Environmental Protection Association
Y. Wang (415) 327-9017
Educates local Chinese American community about environment; exchanges ideas around the Pacific Rim.
...YOU CAN be an environmental information specialist: raise awareness of and concerns about environmental issues.

Committee for Green Foothills
Julia Shepardson (415) 968-7243
Organization that advocates preservation of the natural resources that make our communities a special place to live, work and play. Establishes policies and zoning ordinances that protect the environment.
...YOU CAN volunteer your time to help out with mailings or at events. The committee looks for volunteers with specific environmental interests for special projects.

Magic
David Schrom (415) 323-7333
Programs focusing on ecology and stewardship of the land.
...YOU CAN be an Internet navigational guide: help staff understand the Internet; post and find information.

Physicians for Social Responsibility
Maya Escudero (415) 723-9060
Education about the medical implications of nuclear weapons and nuclear war.
...YOU CAN be a community liaison intern: represent PSR in community events, give presentations.

Santa Clara Valley Audubon Society
Jayne DiCandio (408) 252-3747
Field trips, education programs and advocacy activities
throughout the county.
…YOU CAN join the Environmental Action Committee:
coordinate Audubon's response to environmental issues.

Sierra Club, Loma Prieta Chapter
Kristi Timmings (415) 390-8494
Promotes conservation and offers outdoor activities to members in the Bay Area.
…YOU CAN join the Home Lobby Network: advocate
environmental legislation; call legislators.

Tropical Rainforest Coalition
Alex Rubin (408) 496-9412
Education, conservation and protection of indigenous people
in effort to save rain forests.
…YOU CAN encourage schools to take advantage of the
excellent presentations.

Chapter 7

TAMING THE MEAN STREETS
Keeping Your Neighborhood Safe and Sound

*"Criminals would much rather work
neighborhoods where people are too
indifferent, too busy or too scared to come
out from behind their locked doors."*

—Stephanie Mann
Safe Homes, Safe Neighborhoods

Why Crime Prevention Matters

It is little consolation to many of us that Santa Clara County is one of the safest major metropolitan areas in the U.S. Crime touches us all, directly or indirectly. In fact, the Department of Justice estimates that in a lifetime 98 percent of Americans will be affected by crime at least once, 87 percent more than once. The fastest-growing types of criminal activities in Santa Clara Valley are crimes of violence and property perpetrated by juveniles. Kids with guns are now among the biggest challenges faced by our school systems. Gangs, drugs, and economic despair are root causes of the rise in youth crime. More than anything else, neighborhood crime exemplifies a breakdown in the basic social contracts people write with each other: a failure of community contributes to the sense of alienation, isolation and indifference that permits people to commit crimes against neighbors.

FAST FACTS

- Incidence of crime by juveniles was up 109 percent in Santa Clara County in 1993.
- Gang activity has increased at an alarming rate since 1990.
- Domestic violence is the single greatest cause of injury to women.
- Child abuse affects an estimated 25,000 children annually in Santa Clara County.

Crime costs communities in many ways—fear degrades the quality of life for all, opportunities are lost when people no longer care, property losses and damages demand a personal and psychic toll, crime fighting and punishment require increasing amounts of tax-generated public funds. Fighting crime to keep things from getting worse takes resources away from making things better.

We can use our heads to fight crime by strengthening our community bonds, being good neighbors, targeting at-risk behavior, and by following some commonsense rules. By working in concert with law enforcement officials, schools and organizations offering alternatives, counseling and self-respect to at-risk youths and adults, we can curb violent and property crimes in our corner of the world, stop the merry-go-round of domestic violence, and protect our children from harm.

What You Can Do Right Now
Police-Sponsored Programs

The following community programs are offered by the San Jose Police Crime Prevention Unit (408) 277-4133 (supervisors, Sgt. Ray Barerra and Sgt. Chris Moore). The Unit also makes presentations to businesses, schools and the community; conducts a Ride-Along program; and offers college credit to students in the Intern Program.

► **ORGANIZE THE NEIGHBORHOOD**

Neighborhood Watch was started in the 1970s on the simple premise that neighbors should and can look out for each other. Criminals target homes in neighborhoods where people don't seem to care and where their actions provoke little attention. Show some pride, be visible, work in preventative ways with community policing units, act on any strange behavior and you can keep your streets safer. That's the idea behind the Neighborhood Watch program.

Your impact: Studies show that residential burglaries can be reduced by between 30 and 70 percent when neighbors work together. Other types of crimes also drop dramatically when people practice good neighborhood prevention methods like those provided by Neighborhood Watch.

Where to go

Neighborhood Watch
(408) 277-4133
Ten or more neighbor families meet with police for instruction on neighborhood crime prevention and receive signs and support materials.
…YOU CAN organize your neighbors to deter residential crime and call for a meeting with police representatives.

▶ **ADOPT THE BLOCK**

If, as the old saying goes, it takes an entire village to raise a child, then these days it takes the whole neighborhood to keep a child safe.

The Block Parents program is a coordinated way to provide for the safety of our children. The program works like this: neighbors who sign on as "block parents" agree to provide a "safe house" for local (or any) kids who believe they may be in trouble and come knocking. By displaying the Block Parent sign in windows, kids know that if they are ever followed or accosted by a stranger, they have a secure refuge to run to.

Your impact: You can help save a child from possible assault or abduction by making your home a safe house.

Where to go

Block Parents
(408) 277-4133
Coordinated effort between schools, police and volunteers.
…YOU CAN make your home a "safe house" for children going to and from school or volunteer to start a program at your local school.

► KEEP T.A.B.S. ON KIDS

Residential burglaries in the area have been growing by about 7 percent per year, and more than doubled during the 1980s. Assessing that most burglaries were committed between 8 a.m. and 4 p.m., and that most apprehended perpetrators were of school age, police in San Jose initiated a program in 1981 aimed at keeping kids in school and out of neighbors' houses. Called Truancy Abatement and Burglary Suppression (T.A.B.S.), the program is designed to stop students who are out of class during school hours, detain those without a valid note of explanation at a truancy center, and call the parents or guardian for pick-up. The program has been very effective at deterring young offenders and reducing overall daytime crime.

So successful had been the school-day version of the program, that recently the city of San Jose passed a nighttime curfew law which is aimed at taking juveniles off the streets after 10 p.m. Kids picked up past curfew are taken to the nearest curfew center for processing and parent pick-up.

Your impact: You can help keep young offenders in school, off the streets and at home in the evening by being a T.A.B.S. center volunteer.

Where to go

T.A.B.S.—Truancy Abatement and Burglary Suppression
East Side TABS (408) 926-TABS
West Side TABS (408) 723-TABS
A program to keep kids in school and reduce burglaries. The San Jose curfew law will bring more apprehended teenagers into truancy centers.
…YOU CAN volunteer to work with detained youths and call parents who need to pick up their children.

► PUT A STOP TO IT

The police can never be everywhere at once, but we can help extend their reach by being citizen crime stoppers.

We can do that by reporting a crime when we witness an incident, cooperating with police in solving a witnessed crime, preventing crimes by working to battle apathy, keeping guns out of kids' hands, and blowing the whistle on gang activity.

Your impact: You can send a message to potential lawbreakers that our community cares too much about its quality of life—its security and self-respect—to tolerate criminal activity.

Where to go

City of San Jose Anti-Graffiti Program
Lisa Felde (408) 277-2758
Painting over graffiti immediately discourages it and improves the community.
...YOU CAN be a "Community Graffiti Buster": paint over or remove graffiti in your neighborhood.

Gang Information Hotline
HOTLINE (408) 293-GANG
Confidential hotline for reporting gang-related emergencies or information.

San Jose Crime Stoppers
Officer Roger Malcolm, Coordinator (408) 947-STOP
A nonprofit agency working with San Jose Police providing an anonymous hot-line for tips and information; produces unsolved "Crime of the Week" for news media.
...YOU CAN use the hot-line if you have any information that may be useful to the police in solving a crime. You can also volunteer to help with fundraising, events and publicity.

What You Can Do Right Now
Crisis Intervention Programs

▶ FOR KIDS' SAKE

Children are the most vulnerable victims of crime, either by a stranger or by a parent or loved one. There are nearly 25,000 new cases of child abuse and neglect reported each year in Santa Clara County. Sometimes the best remedy is to remove the children from their homes; other times families resolve their problems and conditions improve. The key is to protect the children from harm; a community must be measured by how safe it is for children.

You can help by volunteering with public and private agencies that reach out to families at risk of abusive behavior and help them work out problems before they turn violent. Whether it's counseling, parent education or housing assistance, there is help available and you can be part of the solution.

Your impact: You can help keep an innocent child from harm by working with the children who have been hurt or removed from their homes, or you can join in the search for a missing child.

| Where to go |

Child Advocacy Council
Candy Pelissoro (415) 327-8120
Prevention of child abuse by strengthening families and removing kids from abusive homes.
…YOU CAN work with kids taken from abusive homes or living in single-parent homes.

Child Quest International
Trish Williams (408) 453-9601
Promote the protection and recovery of missing, abused and exploited children.
…YOU CAN deliver a hands-on safety program to elementary children.

Eastside Neighborhood Center

Carolina Rossman (408) 251-0215

Provides a safe place for youth to gather who might otherwise join a gang.

…YOU CAN help the community become more aware of the center and its services.

Juntos en Cambio (Together Toward Change)

(408) 928-1122

A highly recognized gang prevention program organized by the Mexican American Community Services Agency (MACSA).

…YOU CAN help give kids positive alternatives to gangs and dropping out of school.

Giaretto Institute

Client Services (408) 453-7616

Provides counseling to individuals or groups on issues of child sexual abuse. The Institute works with victims, nonoffending adults and offenders.

…YOU CAN be aware that this resource is available and refer people who may need help.

Odd Fellow-Rebekah Children's Home

Nancy Romer (408) 842-1411

Residential care for neglected or abused children with severe emotional/behavior problems.

…YOU CAN be a recreation program assistant: help with projects and activities; be a friend.

YWCA in Santa Clara County Rape Crisis Center

Child Assault Prevention Coordinator (408) 295-4011 ext. 232

School-based education program offered in various languages, modified for disabled.

…YOU CAN teach children assault prevention techniques through role-playing.

Vanished Children's Alliance

Gisela Bushey (408) 971-4822

Coordinates abduction prevention programs and searches for abducted children.

…YOU CAN be an abduction prevention volunteer: develop and distribute flyers; participate in public events.

▶ WORK WITH THE JUSTICE SYSTEM

When we think of the justice system we most often imagine courtrooms, trials and jails. There is more to it than that; the justice system also works to prevent and remedy crime and help victims. Santa Clara County is home to some highly innovative and imaginative programs that work to break the cycle of crime in the community and reduce the rate and likelihood of repeat offenses.

Your impact: You can work to heal the hurt of victims and change the life path of first-time offenders by volunteering to work with the justice system in our area.

Where to go

Child Advocates of Santa Clara and San Mateo Counties
Susanne Waher (408) 436-6450
Assists children who have been abused or abandoned to deal with the upheaval of court and a new home, new lifestyle.
…YOU CAN be an advocate for an abused child: You could be the youngster's only friend and role model, helping to break the cycle of abuse and provide an example of a healthy, productive lifestyle.

Friends Outside
Jennifer Tait (408) 295-6033
Assists prisoners, ex-prisoners and their families with the immediate and long-term affects of incarceration and acts as a bridge between those served, the community at large and the criminal justice system.
…YOU CAN offer inmates' children opportunities through field trips, individual activities and tutoring. Interview

inmates regarding their special needs—such as locating their children within the system if both parents are in jail, filing court papers, getting medical attention—and follow through. You can also distribute books at county jail via the Friends Outside bookcart or help families of inmates write resumes and sharpen job skills.

Santa Clara County Department of Corrections
Kathy Kleine (408) 299-4005
In charge of the jail system in Santa Clara County.
…YOU CAN help inmates assess their skills, recognize and apply for the right job.

Volunteers in Parole
Susan Carothers (408) 277-1221
Matches youthful offenders who are on parole with attorneys who advise, help them adjust.
…YOU CAN, as an attorney, be a friend, mentor and advisor to one young offender.

Youth Court
Officer Ann Navin (408) 277-4133
Literally a court of peers, Youth Court teaches students about the law and how our justice system works. Based on the knowledge they acquire, members of the youth court determine sentencing for first-time youth offenders. The sentences are community-service-related.
…YOU CAN volunteer your time or resources, or provide information on community programs that need volunteers— opportunities that can be used for the sentencing of first-time offenders.

► DOMESTIC VIOLENCE

Domestic violence is the leading cause of injury for women ages 15 through 44, according to the state of California. Statistics about the frequency of violence against women vary—but not much—from one every 15 seconds to one every four seconds. Nationwide, the American Bar Association estimates that between 3 and 10 million children witness domestic violence in their homes each year. Even when the children themselves are not attacked, they suffer the trauma and bear the lifelong scars of abusive environments. In most cases where violence is taking place in the home, outside intervention is the only hope. You can help.

Santa Clara Valley has a number of exceptional agencies that work with victims, direct and indirect, and offenders of domestic violence. With some minimal training, you can be the source of support to a family in crisis.

Your impact: Whether at a shelter for women and family victims, or on a crisis hot-line, or in the community at large, you can make a major difference in the campaign against domestic violence. Some projects require longer-term commitments, but any amount of time would provide valuable support.

Where to go

Asian Americans for Community Involvement
Help line (408) 975-2739
Shelter for Asian American victims of domestic violence.
…YOU CAN help provide counseling to women and children victims of violence.

Discover Alternatives—La Isla Shelter for victims of domestic violence
Paula Gann (408) 842-3118
Provides shelter for victims of domestic violence.
…YOU CAN help the victims of abuse recover and rebuild their lives.

Mid-Peninsula YWCA
Angela Buenning (415) 494-0972
Multiservice agency addressing family and women's issues: rape, child abuse, child care.

…YOU CAN be a rape crisis hot-line volunteer, providing counseling, advocacy, information and referral to victims.

Next Door, Solutions to Domestic Violence
Kathy Angood, Volunteer Coordinator (408) 279-7550
Emergency shelter for women and children; counseling, education, protection.
…YOU CAN provide shelter and hot-line support: assist counselors at the shelter; answer 24-hour hot-line; organize and staff the Clothes Closet.

Support Network for Battered Women
Michelle Schaeffer (415) 940-7850
Serves women and children who are victims of domestic violence.
…YOU CAN be a crisis line counselor: answer calls from battered women, explain options and services.

Victory Outreach
Rev. Louis Molina (408) 445-3300
A 24-hour residential service providing shelter and counseling for victims of domestic violence.
…YOU CAN work directly with residents who must make often difficult life transitions.

W.A.T.C.H.—Women and Their Children's Housing
Mika Gustavson, Volunteer Coordinator (408) 942-0209
Shelter and empowerment for women and their children to run their own lives free of family violence.
…YOU CAN offer child-care assistance during support groups, help with art projects, homework and playground activities. You can also provide one-on-one peer counseling to assist a mother to develop the social skills necessary to graduate from the program.

Chapter 8

THE SOUL OF THE COMMUNITY
Keeping the Flame of Humanity Lit

"If there is radiance in the soul
it will abound in the family.
If there is radiance in the family
it will be abundant in the community.
If there is radiance in the community
it will grow in the nation.
If there is radiance in the nation
the universe will flourish."

—Lao Tsu

Why the Arts Matter

From the beginning of mankind's adventure on earth, the impulse to share and communicate emotions, ideas and images through artistic expression has run deep in the human spirit. From ancient cave drawings to today's supersophisticated computer graphics, art—in written, lively, and static forms—has been the vehicle for telling our story.

Appreciating art makes us learn and grow in different ways. Art gives a platform for alternate means of expression. Through our support of the arts we can broaden our understanding of the different peoples and perspectives in our diverse community. Art connects us on a deeper level than more mundane forms of communication. Art can serve as a channel for the frustrations and unarticulated angst that otherwise creates friction and conflict in a community. Art is the language of our grace, the torch that illuminates our humanity.

A society expresses its greatness through its arts and letters, and a community expresses its humanity through its support of arts and letters.

We can do ourselves and our community much good by supporting art and artists in Silicon Valley. There are many talented artists and artisans in our midst, and there are many organizations and stages to present both our local talents and to rejoice in the classics.

Silicon Valley is a rich multiculture of mainstream and ethnic arts. Partaking of this colorful panorama is another way to appreciate our diversity, in addition to sustaining fundamental institutions such as symphonies and libraries. And, perhaps most importantly, we can pass the torch of culture on to succeeding generations as we teach our children to appreciate the arts.

What You Can Do Right Now
The Visual Arts and Crafts

Where to go

American Museum of Quilts and Textiles
Margaret Wolverton (408) 971-0323
Unique in the country, showcases quilts and textiles from various cultures and generations.
…YOU CAN coordinate volunteers: work on recruiting, training and planning work schedules and tasks.

de Saisset Museum
Marianne Oswald (408) 554-4528
A free museum of fine art open to all residents and visitors. High quality exhibits.
…YOU CAN be a museum host/hostess: Welcome public, answer questions. Provide security for art.

San Jose Art League
Alexandra Feit (408) 287-8435
Art gallery providing free art experiences for children and adults.

…YOU CAN be a gallery assistant: work in all aspects of gallery management, including teaching children.

San Jose Museum of Art
Rebecca Purdin (408) 294-2787
A well-rounded contemporary arts museum serving Silicon Valley.
…YOU CAN volunteer in a variety of areas: you can be a docent giving guided tours, work in the bookstore, teach in community outreach programs (usually bilingual classes for kindergarten through grade 6), or host receptions.

Triton Museum of Art
(408) 247-3754
A fine arts museum featuring 19th- and 20th-century works.
…YOU CAN be part of the Museum's extensive in-school art outreach program and bring art classes to area public schools.

What You Can Do Right Now
Letters and Learning

| Where to go |

Friends of the Library
(408) 275-1515
Operates Best Friends Bookstore and other fundraising and volunteer activities for San Jose Libraries.
…YOU CAN work in the Bookstore, sort books, organize fundraising events.

Friends of the Los Gatos Library
Mary Kloet (408) 395-5760
Enhances community awareness of library services and sells used books to raise funds.
…YOU CAN assist in attracting members and maintaining lists.

Friends of the Palo Alto Library
(415) 328-1575
A nonprofit association that raises funds for special library purposes and programs through monthly book sales; encourages bequests and donations to the libraries and donations of services for special library projects; and fosters public support of the library and its enrichment.
…YOU CAN volunteer for special events, monthly book sales or mailings, or make a donation to the library. Volunteers with computer and graphic skills are always needed.

Santa Clara County Library
Evelyn Howard (408) 293-2326
Provides library materials for everyone in Santa Clara County.
…YOU CAN be a new book processor: add bar codes and plastic jackets: help books get to shelves quickly.

What You Can Do Right Now
Dance

Where to go

Flamenco Society of San Jose
(408) 971-8468
Showcases the beauty, artistry and culture of flamenco through dance and music.
…YOU CAN use your desktop publishing and typing skills to help translate the beauty of Flamenco.

Las Lupenos de San Jose
Delana Romero (408) 292-0443
Interpreting the full spectacle of Mexican folk culture through dance and theater.
…YOU CAN be an office assistant for bilingual work on computer, telephone and desktop publishing.

San Jose Cleveland Ballet
Tegan McLane (408) 288-2820
Brings world-class dance to the South Bay, making it accessible
to a broad audience.
...YOU CAN be a community liaison: be the voice and face of
the ballet, greet guests, answer phones.

Zohco
Allen Habel (415) 494-8221
Dance training and performances for low-income youth;
builds self-esteem, teamwork, skill.
...YOU CAN design (and manage, if possible) database of
friends, donors, audience.

What You Can Do Right Now
Theater

Where to go

San Jose Civic Light Opera
Margaret Hardy (408) 453-7100
A mixed professional/nonprofessional musical theater group
now in its 60th season, the CLO is the largest subscriber-based
musical theater in the country.
...YOU CAN provide resources to the educational outreach
program, volunteer as a "Describer" for visually impaired
audience members, work with youth activities and fitness
classes.

San Jose Repertory Theatre
Judith Blase (408) 291-2266
Regional professional theater, presenting a full schedule of
presentations each year.

...YOU CAN join the Fund Development Team: acknowledge donors, support events.

San Jose Minority Artists Guild
Arlene Sagun (408) 993-9232
Promotes and presents theatrical performances by various minority arts organizations.
...YOU CAN provide office support and promote awareness of the organization.

San Jose Stage Company
Mary Elizabeth Smith (408) 283-7142
This professional theater company has been operating in San Jose for 12 years.
...YOU CAN be a special assistant to the Executive Director.

Teatro Vision de San Jose
Raul Lozano (408) 947-8227
Latino theater group providing professional bilingual productions in San Jose.
...YOU CAN be a strategic planner: evaluate current organization and develop goals and objectives.

Theatreworks
Jodi Corwin (415) 812-7550
Explores and celebrates the human spirit through innovative works that define our culturally diverse community.
...YOU CAN volunteer in many different capacities including: backstage on crews, at special fundraisers, at different events, or for a number of different programs through an organization called Theatreworkers.

What You Can Do Right Now
Music

Where to go

Friends of Opera, Silicon Valley
Martha Piazza (408) 235-1512
…YOU CAN support the lively art of opera in Silicon Valley
by volunteering to be part of the annual Opera in the Park!
concert held in San Jose, or support any number of other
volunteer opportunities with professional opera companies or
in the schools.

Opera San Jose
Larry Hancock (408) 437-4464
Professional regional opera company located in San Jose
presenting four operas each season in its mainstage subscrip-
tion series.
…YOU CAN volunteer time with the company itself, or assist
in any number of community and in-school music education
and outreach programs.

San Jose Chamber Music Society
Kate Erstein (408) 286-5111
Promotes and educates the public about chamber music;
provides forum for professional musicians.
…YOU CAN support Music for All: bring chamber music to
groups that cannot afford to buy tickets to attend.

San Jose Symphonic Choir
Elisa Spurlin (408) 377-9993
Performs three concerts each year, special engagements with
other area nonprofits.
…YOU CAN be a planning specialist: help in the short- and
long-term planning for the organization.

San Jose Symphony
(408) 287-7383
Nationally recognized, professional symphony ensemble.
…YOU CAN volunteer to help with performances, work with its Youth Orchestra, or participate in any number of community outreach projects.

What You Can Do Right Now
Various and Multimedia Arts

Where to go

Arts Council of Santa Clara County
Virginia Wright (408) 998-2787
The Arts Council champions the arts for the people of Santa Clara County by marshalling for them the greatest possible resources, public and private.
…YOU CAN become a partner in Arts Council activities by making a tax-deductible donation, volunteering with office work or as part of their speaker's bureau.

Asian Heritage Council
Gayle Nishikawa (408) 993-9230
Promotes awareness of Asian American contributions to the arts; encourages Asian artists.
…YOU CAN be a production assistant: assist with events by working on production and marketing.

California Antique Aircraft Museum
Pam Cox (408) 262-8389
Preserves, showcases and teaches about Northern California's rich aviation history.

…YOU CAN be a museum docent: learn about the collection and guide groups through the hangar/museum.

International Institute for the New Classical Arts
Silvia Galvez (408) 942-1473
A new organization promoting arts experiences for kids 8-17.
…YOU CAN be a volunteer planner, fundraiser, or marketing expert.

Jewish Community Center of Greater San Jose
Ken Toren (408) 358-3636
The Center is the focal point for Jewish culture, education, recreation and social activity.
…YOU CAN assist in any one of the Center's many programs.

Mid-Peninsula Access Corp.
Annie Niehaus (415) 494-8686
Enables community groups to use TV for debates, cultural interaction and performances.
…YOU CAN be part of the TV Production Crew: operate the TV studio with direction from staff.

Office of Cultural Affairs, City of San Jose
Donna Pope (408) 277-5144
City agency responsible for coordinating arts and downtown events in San Jose.
…YOU CAN bring the arts to schools where art education budgets have been eliminated.

Palo Alto Cultural Center
Sheila Pastore (415) 329-2370
Art center presents exhibitions, arts programs, studio classes for the community.
…YOU CAN be a Project LOOK! docent: help elementary students to appreciate art, then create their own.

San Jose Historical Museum
Virginia Beck (408) 287-2290
Museum offers a variety of programs including trips to
the museum, Victorian school kids presentation,
Indian school kids presentation, historic transportation
experience and downtown walking tours.
…YOU CAN become a docent, volunteer for any of
the museum programs or help out in the gift shop or
O'Brien's Ice Cream Shop

The Tech Museum of Innovation
Julie Rose (408) 279-7175
A hands-on technology museum and educational
resource for middle school students through adults.
…YOU CAN be an exhibit explainer: interpret and
explain exhibits to school groups and the public.

Villa Montalvo
Kristen Schulz (408) 741-3421
Presents an exciting and interesting series of contemporary art exhibitions throughout the year.
…YOU CAN become involved in the gallery's many
programs as a docent volunteer, as a hospitality
volunteer for their Artist Residency Program or by
helping out at concerts and other special events.

Chapter 9 — **KID STUFF**
Projects to Involve the Whole Family

> *"Children have never been very good at
> listening to their elders, but they have
> never failed to imitate them."*

—James Baldwin

Why Teaching Our Children to Make a Difference Matters

Children learn best by example. If we want to promote among our young the ethic of good citizenship and public service, then we must teach them by example—and by involving them early on. Many of the activities described in this book can be done with your children or young family members. Participation in arts groups, education, helping seniors and disabled persons, and recycling projects are enhanced and given greater impact by involving children. You will be sharing with young people, teaching cultural responsibility, and giving to others. And some of the best quality time you will spend with your kids can come out of such experiences.

At what age should you start kids in community service projects? The answer naturally depends on the individual child and the task at hand. However, it is never too early for a child to share in your example of good works. Many parents I know take their little ones along as they volunteer. Community service can become a routine part of the family week, a tradition that is carried down from one generation to another.

In general, take kids on projects alongside you when they are old enough to, if not help, at least not hinder your efforts. Even if they are too young to fully appreciate the significance of the work you are doing, by being with you they are absorbing the idea of service (children have a built-in grace detector). As they get old enough to do as you do while you're doing it, deputize them and put those youthful energies to work. Later, when they reach an age where doing things with you is "uncool," encourage them to find their own outlets. Even if the go through a stage of rejecting community service in favor of more recreational pursuits, don't worry. Once the die has been cast, the time will come when they will again heed the call to service.

Things Children Can Do to Make a Difference

▶ SORT AND PACK FOOD FOR THE HUNGRY

Second Harvest Food Bank
Beverley Jackson (408) 266-8866
The central clearinghouse for donated food in the county, linking donors and the needy.
ALSO: Organize a school-wide food drive during one week.

▶ PLANT A TREE

Our City Forest
Beth Stochaj (408) 277-3969
Helps schools, neighborhood groups and service clubs plant and care for trees.

▶ WORK WITH HOMEBOUND SENIORS

Friendly Visiting Service
Rita Baum (408) 296-8290
Visits seniors who are home-bound or in nursing homes and have no family support.

▶ MAKE HAPPY TRAILS

Adopt-A-Park
Elizabeth Neves (408) 277-4477
Volunteers provide for the overall maintenance of parks throughout the City of San Jose and other area cities.

Santa Clara County Parks and Recreation Department
Martha Heutel (408) 358-3741
Provides parklands and open space for the enjoyment of
county residents and visitors.

▶ **BE THE SUNSHINE IN SOMEONE'S LIFE**

Peninsula Center for the Blind
Susan Coan (415) 858-0202
Serves the blind and visually impaired in Santa Clara County.

▶ **PARK THE FAMILY CAR**

Silicon Valley Bicycle Coalition
Bill Michel (415) 965-8456
Works for safety, adequate parking and improved conditions
for cyclers.

▶ **CLEAN UP THIS TOWN**

City of San Jose Anti-Graffiti Program
Lisa Felde (408) 277-2758
Painting over graffiti immediately discourages it and improves
the community.

▶ **BE A PET FOSTER PARENT**

Companion Animal Rescue Effort
Brenda Stevens (408) 259-7785
Temporary foster care placement for homeless cats and dogs.

▶ **A HOLIDAY HELPER**

Family Giving Tree
Jennifer Cullenbine (415) 326-1247
Provides food, clothing and assistance to the neediest members
of the community.

Chapter 10

THE MANTLE OF LEADERSHIP
Governing Our Complex Community

"We must be the change we wish to see in the world."

—Mohandas Ghandi

Why Our Participation in Government Matters

Many problems facing our community cannot, of course, be solved in a couple of hours per week. For those willing to make a bigger commitment, there is no more ennobling pursuit than to serve your community in a public capacity.

There are hundreds of elected and appointed government positions in Silicon Valley. There are numerous city and county commissions dealing with a variety of important issues, ranging from arts to housing to parks and traffic problems. And with term limits placed on many offices, the community will need more people to step forward and seek elective office.

Sweeping changes are taking place in local governing bodies with respect to public access to various boards and commissions. For instance, the City of San Jose has depoliticized the application and screening process for boards and commissions under the aegis of "Project Diversity." That makes it easier for women and minorities to win appointments and make a difference.

What You Can Do Right Now
Participatory Government

Some of the most important work of local government is done by citizen committees. Boards and commissions assist in formulating city policies and practices and provide a formal avenue for citizen involvement in city affairs. They also offer a training ground for future leaders of the city.

Your impact: You bring positive action rather than mere criticism to issues about which you have passions or concerns. If you have the energy and commitment, you can make THE difference in how our city, county, state and country run.

What: There are different membership requirements for each board and commission. Please call the city clerk's office in your city for more information. The roster of San Jose commissions follows:

Advisory Commission on Rents
Airport Commission
Arts Commission
Child Care Commission
Civil Service Commission
Code Enforcement Appeals Commission
Committee on Minority, Women and Disadvantaged Business Development
Community Development Block Grant Steering Committee
Council Salary Setting Commission
Deferred Compensation Advisory Committee
Disability Advisory Commission
Federated City Employees Retirement System
Historic Landmarks Commission
Housing Advisory Commission
Human Rights Commission
Library Commission
Mobile Home Advisory Commission
Parking Advisory Commission
Parks and Recreation Commission
Planning Commission
Police and Fire Department Retirement Plan Board of Administration
San Jose Appeals Hearing Board
Senior Citizens' Commission

Suggestion Award Commission
Traffic Appeals Commission
Youth Commission

WHEN TO APPLY:

Thanks to the Project Diversity process in San Jose, openings for commission seats with four-year (and six-year) terms are published during the spring and fall seasons. The Screening Committee reviews all applications received at the City Clerk's Office and makes recommendations to the City Council's Rules Committee. The Rules Committee conducts interviews and makes final recommendations to City Council.

Notices Published	Aug. 1	Jan. 22
Application Deadline	Oct. 1	Apr. 1
Screening Committee Interviews	Nov. 11-29	May 20-June 7
Recommendations to Council Liaison	Dec. 2	June 10
Rules Committee Recommendations	Dec. 9	June 17
Council Approves Recommendations	Dec. 16	June 24

Where to go

City Clerk's Office, City of San Jose, Room 116
801 North First St., San Jose 95110
(408) 277-4424

Call your city for available boards and commissions:
CITIES IN SANTA CLARA COUNTY

City of Campbell
70 N. First Street, Campbell 95008
City Clerk's Office (408) 866-2117

City of Cupertino
10300 Torre Avenue, Cupertino 95014
City Clerk's Office (408) 777-3223

City of Los Altos
1 N. San Antonio Road, Los Altos 94022
City Offices (415) 948-1491

Town of Los Altos Hills
26379 Fremont Road, Los Altos Hills 94022
Town Hall (415) 941-7222

City of Milpitas
455 E. Calaveras Boulevard, Milpitas 95035
General Information (408) 942-2310

City of Monte Sereno
18041 Saratoga-Los Gatos Road, Monte Sereno 95030
City Offices (408) 354-7635

City of Morgan Hill
17555 Peak Avenue, Morgan Hill 95037
City Offices (408) 779-7271

City of Mountain View
500 Castro Street, Mountain View 94041
City Offices (415) 903-6300

City of Palo Alto
250 Hamilton Avenue, Palo Alto 94301
City Offices (415) 329-2571

City of Santa Clara
1500 Warburton Avenue, Santa Clara 95050
Administrative Offices (408) 984-3000

City of Saratoga
13777 Fruitvale Avenue, Saratoga 95070
City Offices (408) 867-3438

City of Sunnyvale
456 W. Olive Avenue, Sunnyvale 94088-3707
Offices of the City Manager (408) 730-7533

COUNTY BOARDS AND COMMISSIONS

Santa Clara County posts notices for openings of three- and four-year terms on boards and commissions on the back of the agenda of each meeting of the County Board of Supervisors. These notices are also posted in the first-floor lobby of the County Building. The term expires for many positions on June 30 of each year, but others become available throughout the year. Candidate applications are distributed to the Board of Supervisors, and each Supervisor contacts candidates for boards or commissions in which he or she is involved. Call your County Supervisor's office for more information.

What: The roster of County of Santa Clara boards and commissions follows:

Ad Hoc Committee on Transportation for the Mobility Impaired
Advisory Commission on Persons with Disabilities
Airports Commission
Alcohol and Drug Advisory Board
Animal Advisory Commission
Assessment Appeals Boards I & II
Bicycle Advisory Committee
Code Enforcement Board of Appeals
Consumer Affairs Advisory Commission
Correctional Industries Advisory Board
County Justice System Advisory Board
Domestic Violence Council
Emergency Medical Care Commission
Council on Equal Employment Opportunities
Fair Association Board of Directors
Fish and Game Commission
Florence Sister-County Commission
Historical Heritage Commission
Commission on HIV and AIDS
Human Relations Commission
Library Commission

Local Agency Formation Commission
Maternal, Child and Adolescent Health Board
Mental Health Advisory Board
National Guard and Veterans Affairs Commission
Parks and Recreation Commission
Personnel Board
Planning Commission
Plumber Board of Examiners
Private Industry Council
San Martin Planning Committee
Self-Esteem Task Force
Senior Care Commission
Social Services Advisory Commission
Commission on the Status of Women
Transportation Commission
Youth Commission

Where to go

Clerk of the Santa Clara Board of Supervisors
70 West Hedding Street, San Jose 95113
(408) 299-4321

▶ KEEP IN TOUCH

Call or write to your city or town council representative, state legislator, congressional representative or U.S. senator. Let them know you care and are willing to be involved. A legislative rule of thumb: every letter represents 100 constituents. Ten letters can create a groundswell of action.

▶ RUN FOR ELECTIVE OFFICE

For the stout of heart and truly committed, standing for public office can be one of the most effective ways to make a difference in our community. From school boards to Congress, there are numerous offices that influence public policy and practice and help shape the quality of life in Silicon Valley. Again, however, the time commitment is significant, ranging from several days a week for a school board member to full-time job (and then some) for state and federal legislators.

Is running for public office right for you? Only you can be the judge of that.

Are you right for public office? Ultimately, your neighbors will decide that in the elective process. It is important to note, however, that there are very few systemic barriers to your running for office. Even if you have no experience, or never dreamed of being a candidate, don't rule out public office as an option. You don't have to be a professional politician to enter the arena—and these days, it is to your advantage not to be a professional. With term limits being invoked, the political process is being opened up to broader citizen participation. If you think you can add value and make a difference in a public capacity, contact the Registrar of Voters to get more information.

| Where to go |

Santa Clara County Registrar of Voters
(408) 298-7400

What You Can Do Right Now
Community Leadership

▶ **DEVELOP YOUR LEADERSHIP SKILLS**

You can gain experience for these challenging government appointments through all varieties of service to the community and by learning specific leadership skills in any of several local leadership programs. Many leadership programs serve particular constituencies in our community, such as youth or minorities.

Your impact: Acquiring skills from these programs can greatly enhance your effectiveness at any of the challenging and influential positions available in both the public and private sectors.

| Where to go |

Leadership San Jose
Sunny Clagget (408) 291-5267

Santa Clara Valley Leadership Program
Focused on minorities and women.
Sujatha Suresh (408) 452-8181

California Leadership
Mitch Saunders, Director of Programs (408) 438-8350

Leadership Sunnyvale
Anne Hines, Director (408) 738-0846

California Association of Leadership Programs
Donna Brown (408) 733-4032

► NEIGHBORHOOD ASSOCIATIONS

Often those closest to a problem can provide—or at least identify—the best solutions. That is clearly the strength of the growing ranks of neighborhood associations that have sprung up in Santa Clara Valley. Responding to both the unique character and needs of the smaller communities within our wider Valley community, neighborhood associations have united and galvanized neighbors and taken their energies and voices directly to City Hall, and are getting action. Traffic problems, crime and other service needs are frequently the biggest concerns. …YOU CAN make a difference close to home by joining and attending meetings of your local neighborhood association. Below is a list of selected associations. If your neighborhood doesn't have an association, any one of the following groups can tell you how to start one.

24th Street Neighborhood Association
172 N. 24th Street
San Jose 95116

Almaden Valley Community Association
P. O. Box 20056
San Jose 95160

Berryessa Citizens Advisory Council
1146 Colonial Lane
San Jose 95132

Brookwood Terrace Neighborhood Association
P. O. Box 83
San Jose 95103-0083

Buena Vista Neighborhood Association
1757 W. San Carlos Street, #100
San Jose 95128

Canoas Garden Neighborhood Association
P. O. Box 36146
San Jose 95158

Jackson-Taylor Neighborhood Association
55 E. Empire Street
San Jose 95112

Market/Almaden Neighborhood Association
P. O. Box 90358
San Jose 95109

Meadows Association
P. O. Box 36132
San Jose 95125

Monta Loma Neighborhood Association
P. O. Box 382
Mountain View 94042

Northside Residents Association
P. O. Box 4454
Santa Clara 95054

Roosevelt Park Community Action Team
901 E. Santa Clara Street
San Jose 95116

RoseGlen Neighborhood Association
P. O. Box 28642
San Jose 95159

Shadowbrook I Homeowners Association
P. O. Box 20271
San Jose 95160

Shasta/Hanchett Park Neighborhood Association
P. O. Box 28251
San Jose 95159

Sunnyhills Improvement Association
P. O. Box 361321
Milpitas 95136

Villa De Santa Teresa Homeowners Association
P. O. Box 1312
Coyote 95013

West Side Community Crusaders
P. O. Box 10261
San Jose 95127

Willow Glen Neighborhood Association
P. O. Box 7706
San Jose 95150

Woodside of Almaden Homeowners
P. O. Box 20601
San Jose 95160

▶ NONPROFIT GOVERNANCE

There are more than 2,500 nonprofit organizations in Santa Clara County alone, all striving to succeed and make a difference in the lives of those they serve. Some are large and successful, able to generate funds from grant makers, support from individuals and community visibility for their causes. Others are smaller, less well-known and often struggling to meet the challenges they have accepted as a part of their mission. Each of these organizations is governed by a board of directors that represents the community, i.e., the shareholders or stakeholders in the success of the enterprise.

Your impact: Board members monitor the activities of the organizations, help them raise funds, tell friends and acquaintances about their accomplishments and broaden and heighten the reach of each organization by their service on the board. Serving on the board of a nonprofit organization is one of the hardest jobs any of us will ever do, but one that gives an incredible sense of accomplishment and making a difference.

Where to go |

The Board Connection
Germaine Cummings (408) 244-0440
The Board Connection links exceptional people from diverse communities with nonprofit organization governing boards in Santa Clara County. The program provides new board members with a realistic introduction to board roles and responsibilities. It works with the nonprofit organizations to ensure a mutually successful placement. And the program is unique in the ongoing training and support it provides to both individuals and organizations after the placement is made.

Chapter 11

THE ONE-MINUTE CITIZEN
Things Even the Busiest People Can Do to Make a Difference

*"I am only one
But still I am one
I cannot do everything
But still I can do something"*

—Edward Everett Hale

Okay, so this isn't a good time in your life to dedicate even two hours in a week to community service. You can still make a difference with the things you do (and don't do) on a daily basis.

In a matter of minutes you can:

▶ **REGISTER TO VOTE**
Santa Clara County Registrar of Voters
(408) 298-7400
Remember to reregister whenever you changes addresses.

▶ **VOTE**
The location of your polling place will come in the mail with your sample ballot, or call the Registrar of Voters.
(408) 298-7400

▶ **WRITE TO THE PRESIDENT**
The Honorable William J. Clinton
President of the United States
Executive Office of the President
1600 Pennsylvania Avenue, N.W.
Washington, D.C. 20500

OR...

▶ **FAX THE PRESIDENT**
(202) 456-2883

OR...

▶ **E-MAIL THE PRESIDENT**
President@WhiteHouse.gov

OR...

▶ **CALL THE PRESIDENT**
(202) 456-1111

▶ **PULL A FAST ONE ON HUNGER**
Take one of the "Food for all" tags at the check-out register of participating Nob Hill and Lucky stores. For increments of $1, $2 or $5 you can help feed the hungry through 30 different local charities.

▶ **WRITE A CHECK**
Nonprofits need financial resources to do their good work. Take a moment and write a check to your favorite charitable organization.

OR...

▶ **DO IT THE UNITED WAY**
Sign up for United Way payroll deductions at work:
The United Way of Santa Clara County
1992 The Alameda
San Jose 95126
(408) 247-1200

OR...

▶ **JUST SAY CHARGE IT**
Call up and make a donation via a credit card. Most nonprofits

today will be more than happy to give you credit for credit.

OR...

▶ **CHARGE WITH PURPOSE**

Use an "affinity card" to make everyday purchases and your donation is made by the card company to the designated charity. Contact your favorite charity to see if they participate in this program.

▶ **INVEST IN SILICON VALLEY**

Ask your broker to create a "Silicon Valley" growth fund for you, including a portfolio of growth stocks, "blue chips," state, municipal and local corporate bonds.

▶ **SAVE OUR WATER**

We are never far enough away from the next drought to ever let down our guard. Save precious water by installing low-flow faucets and shower heads throughout your home (the average shower uses 40 gallons of water), and be sure to shut off the faucet while you brush your teeth or shave (a running faucet wastes 3 to 5 gallons of water every minute).

▶ **FIGHT CRIME WITHOUT EVER LEAVING HOME**

Reduce neighborhood crime by keeping a look-out for strangers or strange behavior: when in doubt, call the police.

▶ **REDUCE LANDFILL WASTE**

Reduce waste by bringing a mug to work—instead of using paper or Styrofoam cups.

▶ **BE IN-KIND TO YOUR NEIGHBORS**

Donate your product to a fundraising auction

▶ **BUY LOCAL AREA SOFTWARE**

Buy software created by local companies.

▶ **SIGN A PETITION**

At least read one. Get to know what your neighbors care deeply about.

▶ **LET YOUR FINGERS DO THE DRIVING**

Use the telephone to locate a desired item (rather than driving around).

▶ **THAT'S THE TICKET!**

Give unused tickets back to local theater and arts groups for resale or as free tickets to students.

▶ **SOLD! TO SANTA**

Buy holiday gifts through charity auctions.

▶ **JUST DESSERTS**

Eat at restaurants that participate in the "Second Helping" program.

▶ **BUY LOCAL AREA HARDWARE**

Buy locally produced computer hardware.

▶ **GIVE SOMEONE A CHANCE**

Hire a physically challenged employee or "temp."

▶ **VISIT AN AREA MUSEUM**

Visit a museum. Purchase holiday gifts at local museum shops.

▶ **LATE GREAT BOOKS**

Give old books to libraries for booksale fundraisers.

Afterword
A Personal Word About Volunteering

"I feel good when I do good."

—Abraham Lincoln

I don't know about you, but I'm always busy. There never seems to be enough time to do it all—work, take care of my children, help my extended family, make time for fun. Sound familiar? Between meetings, airline flights and reading to my kids, my life is truly a scheduling challenge. Yet somehow I've always managed to find time for volunteering and civic activities. I think part of the reason is a sense of duty: I live in a community that has needs; if I can help, I'm obliged to do so. Another part of the reason is more selfish: I like rolling up my sleeves and helping out—it makes me feel good when I make a difference.

How'd I get hooked on volunteering? I did all the usual things growing up: Boy Scouts, food drives, Christmas caroling at senior centers, and so on. About the time I got to high school, however, I got really involved. When I was 17, I worked after school as a community organizer, and even led a major campaign—successfully—to build a new high school in my hometown. Through these and other efforts I met a lot of people who were hurting. I'll never forget the man I met who lived on nothing but a bottle of ketchup in the last week each month before his next Social Security check arrived. He'd occasionally offer me a cup of "ketchup soup." Hundreds of stories like that can get to you.

And yet, I grew up with very little myself. I was raised in a single-parent home without a lot of money (technically, we were poor, but I've always believed being "poor" is a state of mind—I never let myself be poor). Part of the reason why my brother and sisters and I never noticed how little we had was that my mother was (and still is) a social worker for the Commonwealth of Massachusetts. While we were growing up, she would occasionally share with us some pretty powerful stories from her caseload of people in real need. It tended to put our life in a different perspective.

In college I worked as an intern for Governor Michael Dukakis. My assignment was the Office of Community Services—through which all the real and extreme cases of need came to the governor's attention. Talk about your eye-opening experiences. Again, if I ever felt down, I just needed to look at the people who came to me every day in order to get real.

That's the powerful thing about volunteering in the community—it gives your life alternate reference points.

I keep off that little hamster wheel of corporate life by keeping other points of reference in plain sight. Since I was a kid I've found that by working in the community I keep track of what's important—and what's not.

When you start to think the world revolves around your work, your profitability ratios, your market share penetration, your sales quotas, it's time for a dose of reality. Time to sort some donated food at Second Harvest. Do some painting at a children's shelter. Listen to a lonely senior's personal story. Teach a new friend to read. Give someone hope.

I countervail life's little moments of imbalance by getting out there and doing something completely different. When you volunteer you see the world in a new way, realize how good you've really got it, make the world a better place and feel good about yourself. That's why it is my belief that the volunteer gets the biggest benefit out of volunteering. I am not alone. Study after study shows that people who round out their lives by performing community service live happier, healthier lives. People who volunteer are often the best types of employees.

Volunteer to do something good. Volunteer for yourself. When you see it that way, you'll be surprised how much time in your hectic life you can free up for making a difference.

Appendix

OTHER RESOURCES

The following umbrella organizations are excellent resources and can benefit from your support:

CompuMentor
(415) 512-7784
Helps nonprofit organizations solve their computer needs. In the past few years, CompuMentor has assisted more than 600 nonprofits.

Design Response
Daisy Meyer (408) 244-2479
Designs office space and secures corporate donations of furniture for nonprofits.
Interior designers—please apply: public service liaison needed to pick up donated furniture with a hearty "thank you" and bring to storage.

Joint Venture: Silicon Valley Network
99 Almaden Boulevard, Suite 620
San Jose 95113-2002
Telephone (408) 271-7213
Facsimile (408) 271-7214
E-mail: jvsvoffice@aol.com
Community-wide organization aimed at revitalizing Silicon Valley's economy and competitiveness.

Junior League of San Jose
(408) 264-3058
Junior League of Palo Alto • Mid Peninsula
(415) 321-5026
Trains young women for leadership in the community and places them in volunteer jobs. Membership is open to all who demonstrate a desire to volunteer, work hard and learn.

The Nonprofit Development Center
1922 The Alameda, Suite 212
San Jose 95126
Telephone (408) 452-8181
Facsimile (408) 452-0231

The Resource Area For Teachers (The RAFT)
Mary Simon (408) 559-1231
A new nonprofit organization in the Bay Area that will pull in volunteers from all sections of the community and collect industries' reusable and/or nonrecyclable discard items, which will be available to teachers in our community.

Retired Seniors Volunteer Program—R.S.V.P.
(408) 277-4790 or (415) 321-7232
Local chapters of a national organization linking people aged 55 and over with volunteer opportunities in a broad range of nonprofit areas.

The Silicon Valley Charity Ball Foundation
Susan Currie (415) 941-8444
The largest annual, one-night black-tie fundraiser in the San Francisco Bay Area. A nonprofit organization comprised of community and business leaders, has raised more than $3 million for 141 different Santa Clara County charities.